DISCOURSES
ON THE BHAGAVAT GITA

DISCOURSES

ON THE BHAGAVAT GITA

To help Students in Studying its philosophy.

Mr. T. SUBBA ROW, B. A., B.L., F.T.S.

GYAN

Published by

Gyan Publishing House
5, Ansari Road
Daryaganj, New Delhi-110002
Phone: 011-47034999, 9811692060
E-mail: books@gyanbooks.com

Distribution Network
gyanbooks.com
India, USA, Canada, UK, Australia, France

ISBN: 978-81-212-9364-8 (PB)
First Published, 1888

2nd Impression 2023

Printed at: Gyan Press, Delhi.

DISCOURSES ON THE BHAGAVAT GITA

AUTHOR: Mr. T. SUBBA ROW

The Theosophical Society's Publications.

ॐ

DISCOURSES

ON THE BHAGAVAT GITA.

To help stu lents in studying its philosophy.

BY

Mr. T. SUBBA ROW, B. A., B. L., F.T.S.

PRINTED FOR THE BOMBAY
THEOSOPHICAL PUBLICATION FUND.

BY

TOOKARAM TATYA.

BOMBAY:
PRINTED AT THE JOINT-STOCK PRINTING PRESS.

1888.

INTRODUCTION.

In studying the Bhagavad Gita it must not be treated as if isolated from the rest of the Mahabharata as it at present exists. It was inserted by Vyasa in the right place with special reference to some of the incidents in that book. One must first realise the real position of Arjuna and Krishna in order to appreciate the teaching of the latter. Among other appellations Arjuna has one very strange name—he is called at different times by ten or eleven names, most of which are explained by himself in Virataparva. One name is omitted from the list, *i. e.*, Nara. This word simply means "man." But why a particular man should be called by this as a proper name may at first sight appear strange. Nevertheless herein lies a clue which enables us to understand not only the position of the Bhagavad Gita in the text and its connection with Arjuna and Krishna, but the entire current running through the whole of the Mahabharata, implying Vyasa's real views of the origin, trials and destiny of man. Vyasa looked upon Arjuna as man, or rather the real monad in man; and upon Krishna as the Logos, or the spirit that comes to save man. To some it appears strange that this highly philosophical teaching should have been inserted in a place apparently utterly unfitted for it. The discourse is alleged to have taken place between Arjuna and Krishna just before the battle began to rage. But when once you begin to appreciate the Mahabharata, you will see this was the fittest place for the Bhagavad Gita.

Historically the great battle was a struggle between two families. Philosophically it is the great battle, in which the human spirit has to fight against the lower passions in the physical body. Many of our readers have probably heard about the so-called Dweller on the Threshold, so vividly described in Lytton's novel "Zanoni." According to this author's description, the Dweller on the Threshold seems to be some elemental, or other monster of mysterious form, appearing before the neophyte just as he is about to enter the mysterious land, and attempting to shake his resolution with menaces of unknown dangers if he is not fully prepared.

There is no such monster in reality. The description must be taken in a figurative sense. But nevertheless there is a Dweller on the Threshold, whose influence on the mental plane is far more trying than any physical terror can be. The real Dweller on the Threshold is formed of the despair and despondency of the neophyte, who is called upon to give up all his old affections for kindred, parents and children, as well as his aspirations for objects of wordly ambition, which have perhaps been his associates for many incarnations. When called upon to give up these things, the neophyte feels a kind of blank, before he realises his higher possibilities. After having given up all his associations, his life itself seems to vanish into thin air. He seems to have lost all hope, and to have no object to live and work for. He sees no signs of his own future progress. All before him seems darkness ; and a sort of pressure comes upon the soul, under which it begins to droop, and in most cases he begins to fall back and gives up further progress. But in the case of a man who really struggles, he will battle against that despair, and be able to proceed on the Path. I may here refer you to a few passages in Mill's autobiography. Of course the author knew nothing of occultism ; but there was one stage in his mental life, which seems to have come on at a particular point of his career and to have closely resembled what I have been describing. Mill was a great analytical philosopher. He made an exhaustive analysis of all mental processes,—mind, emotions, and will.

"I now saw or thought I saw, what I had always before received with incredulity,—that the habit of analysis has a tendency to wear away the feelings, as indeed it has when no other mental habit is cultivated. * * * Thus neither selfish nor unselfish pleasures were pleasures to me."

At last he came to have analysed the whole man into nothing. At this point a kind of melancholy came over him, which had something of terror in it. In this state of mind he continued for some years, until he read a copy of Wordsworth's poems full of sympathy for natural objects and human life. "From them," he says, "I seemed to learn what would be the perennial sources of happiness, when all the greater evils of life should have been removed." This feebly indicates what the chela must experience when he has determined to renounce all old associates, and is called to live for a bright future on a higher plane. This transition stage was more or less the position of Arjuna before the discourse in question. He was about to engage in a war of extermination against foes led by some of his nearest relations, and he not unnaturally shrank from the thought of killing kindred and friends. We are each of us called upon to kill out all our passions and desires, not that they are all necessarily evil in themselves, but that their influence must be annihilated before we can establish ourselves on the higher planes. The position of Arjuna is intended to typify that of a chela, who is called upon to face the Dweller on the Threshold. As the guru prepares his chela for the trials of initiation by philosophical teaching, so at this critical point Krishna proceeds to instruct Arjuna.

The Bhagavad Gita may be looked upon as a discourse addressed by a guru to a chela who has fully determined upon the renunciation of all worldly desires and aspirations, but yet feels a certain despondency, caused by the apparent blankness of his existence. The book contains eighteen chapters, all intimately connected. Each chapter describes a particular phase or aspect of human life. The student should bear this in mind in reading the book, and endeavour to work out the correspondences. He will find what appear to be unnecessary repetitions. These were a necessity of the method adopted by Vyasa, his intention being to represent nature in different ways, as seen from the standpoints of the various philosophical schools which flourished in India,

As regards the moral teaching of the Bhagavad Gita, it is often asserted by those who do not appreciate the benefits of occult study, that, if everybody pursued this course, the world would come to a standstill; and, therefore, that this teaching can only be useful to the few, and not to ordinary people. This is not so. It is of course true that the majority of men are not in the position to give up their duties as citizens and members of families. But Krishna distinctly states that these duties, if not reconcilable with ascetic life in a forest, can certainly be reconciled with that kind of mental abnegation which is far more powerful in the production of effects on the higher planes than any physical separation from the world. For though the ascetic's body may be in the jungle, his thoughts may be in the world. Krishna therefore teaches that the real importance lies not in physical but in mental isolation. Every man who has duties to discharge must devote his mind to them. But, says the teacher, it is one thing to perform an action as a matter of duty, and another thing to perform the same from inclination, interest, or desire. It is thus plain that it is in the power of a man to make definite progress in the development of his higher faculties, whilst there is nothing noticea ble in his mode of life to distinguish him from his fellows. No religion teaches that men should be the slaves of interest and desire Few inculcate the necessity of seclusion and asceticism. The great objection that has been brought against Hinduism and Buddhism is that by recommending such a mode of life to students of occultism they tend to render void the lives of men engaged in ordinary avocations. This objection however rests upon a misapprehension. For these religions teach that it is not the nature of the act, but the mental attitude of its performer, that is of importance. This is the moral teaching that runs through the whole of the Bhagavad Gita. The reader should note carefully the various arguments by which Krishna establishes his proposition. He will find an account of the origin and destiny of the human monad, and of the manner in which it attains salvation through the aid and enlightenment derived from its Logos. Some have taken Krishna's exhortation to Arjuna to worship him alone as supporting the doctrine of a personal god. But this is an erroneous conclusion. For, though speaking of himself as Parabrahm, Krishna is still the Logos. He describes himself as Atma, but no doubt is one with Parabrahm, as there is no essential difference between Atma and Parabrahm. Certainly the Logos can speak of itself as Parabrahm. So all sons of God, including Christ, have spoken of themselves as one with the Father. His saying that he exists in almost every entity in the Cosmos, expresses strictly an attribute of Parabrahm. But a Logos, being manifestation of Parabrahm, can use these words and assume these attributes. Thus Krishna only calls upon Arjuna to worship his own highest spirit, through which alone he can hope to attain salvation. Krishna is teaching Arjuna what the Logos in the course of initiation will teach the human monad, pointing out that through himself alone is salvation to be obtained. This implies no idea of a personal god.

Again notice the view of Krishna respecting the Sankhya philosophy. Some strange ideas are afloat about this system. It is supposed that the Sutras we possess represent the original aphorisms of Kapila. But this has been denied by many great teachers, including Sankaráchárya, who say that they do not represent his real views, but those of some other Kapila, or the writer of the book. The real Sankhya philosophy is identical with the Pythagorean system of numerals, and the philosophy embodied in the Chaldean system of numbers. The philosopher's object was to represent all the mysterious powers of nature by a few simple formulæ, which he expressed in numerals. The original book is not to be found, though it is possible that it still exists. The system now put forward under this name contains little beyond an account of the evolution of the elements and a few combinations of the same which enter into the formation of the various tatwams. Krishna reconciles the Sankhya philosophy, Raj Yog, and even Hatta Yog, by first pointing out that the philosophy, if properly understood, leads to the same merging of the human monad in the Logos. The doctrine of Karma, which embraces a wider field than that allowed it by orthodox pundits, who have limited its signification solely to religious observances, is the same in all philosophies, and is made by Krishna to include almost every good and bad act or even thought. The student must first go through the Bhagavad Gita and next try to differentiate the teachings in the eighteen different parts under different categories. He should observe how these different aspects branch out from one common centre, and how the teachings in these chapters are intended to do away with the objections of different philosophers to the occult theory and the path of salvation here pointed out. If this is done, the book will show the real attitude of occultists in considering the nature of the Logos and the human monad. In this way almost all that is held sacred in different systems is combined. By such teaching Krishna succeeds in dispelling Arjuna's despondency and in giving him a higher idea of the nature of the force acting through him, though for the time being it is manifesting itself as a distinct individual. He overcomes Arjuna's disinclination to fight by analysing the idea of self, and showing that the man is in error, who thinks that *he* is doing this, that and the other. When it is found that what he calls "I" is a sort of fiction, created by his own ignorance, a great part of the difficulty has ceased to exist. He further proceeds to demonstrate the existence of a higher individuality, of which Arjuna had no previous knowledge. Then he points out that this individuality is connected with the Logos. He furthermore expounds the nature of the Logos and shows that it is Parabrahm. This is the substance of the first eleven or twelve chapters. In those that follow Krishna gives Arjuna further teaching in order to make him firm of purpose; and explains to him how, through the inherent qualities of Prakriti and Purusha, all the entities have been brought into existence.

It is to be observed that the number eighteen is constantly recurring in the Mahabharata, seeing that it contains eighteen Parvas, the contending armies were divided into eighteen army-corps, the battle raged eighteen days, and the book is called by a name which means eighteen. This number is mysteriously connected with Arjuna. I have been describing him as man, but even Parabrahm manifests itself as a Logos in more ways than one. Krishna may be the Logos, but only one particular form of it. The number eighteen is to represent this particular form. Krishna is the Logos that overshadows the human Ego and his gift of his sister in marriage to Arjuna typifies the union between the light of the Logos and the human monad. It is worthy of note that Arjuna did not want Krishna to fight for him, but only to act as his charioteer and to be his friend and counsellor. From this it will be perceived that the human monad must fight its own battle, assisted, when once the human being begins to tread the true path, by his own Logos.

NOTES ON THE BHAGAVAD GITA.

I.

Before proceeding with the subject, I think it necessary to make a few preliminary remarks. All of you know that our Society is established upon a cosmopolitan basis. We are not wedded to any particular creed or to any particular system of religious philosophy. We consider ourselves as mere enquirers. Every great system of philosophy is brought before us for the purpose of investigation. At the present time we are not at all agreed upon any particular philosophy which could be preached as the philosophy of our Society. This is no doubt a very safe position to take at the commencement. But from all this it does not follow that we are to be enquirers and enquirers only. We shall, no doubt, be able to find out the fundamental principles of all philosophy and base upon them a system which is likely to satisfy our wants and aspirations. You will kindly bear this in mind, and not take my views as the views of the Society, or as the views of any other authority higher than myself. I shall simply put them forward for what they are worth. They are the results of my own investigations into various systems of philosophy and no higher authority is alleged for them. It is only with this view that I mean to put forward the few remarks I have to make.

You will remember that I gave an introductory lecture the last time we met here, and pointed out to you the fundamental notions which ought to be borne in mind in trying to understand the Bhagavad Gita. I need not recapitulate all that I then said; it will be simply necessary to remind you that Krishna was intended to represent the *Logos*, which I shall hereafter explain at length; and that Arjuna, who was called *Nara*, was intended to represent the human monad.

The Bhagavad Gita, as it at present stands, is essentially practical in its character and teachings, like the discourses of all religious teachers who have appeared on the scene of the world to give a few practical directions to mankind for their spiritual guidance. Just as the sayings of Christ, the discourses of Buddha, and the preachings of various other philosophers which have come down to us, are essentially didactic in character and practical in their tone, so is the Bhagavad Gita. But these teachings will not be understood— indeed, in course of time they are even likely to be misunderstood—unless their basis is constantly kept in view. The Bhagavad Gita starts from certain premises, which are not explained at length,—they are simply alluded to here and there, and quoted for the purpose of enforcing the doctrine, or as authorities, and Krishna does not go into the details of the philosophy which is their foundation. Still there is a philosophical basis beneath his teachings, and unless that basis is carefully surveyed, we cannot understand the practical applications of the teachings of the Bhagavad Gita, or even test them in the only way in which they can be tested.

Before proceeding further, I find it absolutely necessary to preface my discourse with an introductory lecture, giving the outlines of this system of philosophy which I have said is the basis of the practical teaching of Krishna. This philosophy I cannot gather or deduce from the Bhagavad Gita itself; but I can show that the premises with which it starts are therein indicated with sufficient clearness.

This is a very vast subject, a considerable part of which I cannot at all touch; but I shall lay down a few fundamental principles which are more or less to be considered as axiomatic in their character—you may call them postulates for the time being—so many as are absolutely necessary for the purpose of understanding the philosophy of the Bhagavad Gita. I shall not attempt to prove every philosophical principle I am about to lay down in the same manner in which a modern scientist attempts to prove all the laws he has gathered from an examination of nature.

In the case of a good many of these principles, inductive reasoning and experiment are out of the question; it will be next to impossible to test them in the ordinary course of life or in the ways available to the generality of mankind. But, nevertheless, these principles do rest upon very high authority. When carefully explained, they will be found to be the basis of every system of philosophy which human intellect has ever constructed, and furthermore, will also be found,—I venture to promise—to be perfectly consistent with all that has been found out by man in the field of science; at any rate they give us a working hypothesis—a hypothesis which we may safely adopt at the commencement of our labours,—for the time being. This hypothesis may be altered if you are quite certain that any new facts necessitate its alteration, but at any rate it is a working hypothesis which seems to explain all the facts which it is necessary for us to understand before we proceed upon a study of the gigantic and complicated machinery of nature.

Now to proceed with this hypothesis. First of all, I have to point out to you that any system of practical instruction for spiritual guidance will have to be judged, first, with reference to the nature and condition of man and the capabilities that are locked up in him; secondly, with reference to the cosmos and the forces to which man is subject and the circumstances under which he has to progress.

Unless these two points are sufficiently investigated, it will be hardly possible for us to ascertain the highest goal that man is capable of reaching; and unless there is a definite aim or a goal to reach, or an ideal towards which man has to progress, it will be almost impossible to say whether any particular instruction is likely to conduce to the welfare of mankind or not. Now I say these instructions can only be understood by examining the nature of the cosmos, the nature of man, and the goal towards which all evolutionary progress is tending.

Before I proceed farther, let me tell you that I do not mean to adopt the sevenfold classification of the principles in man that has up to this time been adopted in Theosophical writings generally. Just as I would classify the principles in man, I would classify the principles in the solar system and in the cosmos. There is a certain amount of similarity and the law of correspondence—as it is called by some writers—whatever may be the reason,—is the law which obtains in a good many of the phenomena of nature, and very often by knowing what happens in the case of the microcosm we are enabled to infer what takes place in that of the macrocosm. Now as regards the numbers of principles and their relation between themselves, this sevenfold classification which I do not mean to adopt, seems to me to be a very unscientific and misleading one. No doubt the number seven seems to play an important part in the cosmos, though it is neither a power nor a spiritual force; but it by no means necessarily follows that in every case we must adopt that number. What an amount of confusion has this sevenfold classification given rise to! These seven principles, as generally enumerated, do not correspond to any natural lines of cleavage, so to speak, in the constitution of man. Taking the seven principles in the order in which they are generally given, the physical body is separated from the so-called life-principle; the latter from what is called *linga sarira* (very often confounded with *sukshma sarira.*) Thus the physical body is divided into three principles. Now here we may make any number of divisions ; if you please, you may as well enumerate nerve-force, blood, and bones, as so many distinct parts, and make the number of divisions as large as sixteen or thirty-five. But still the physical body does not constitute a separate entity apart from the life principle, nor the life principle apart from the physical body, and so with the *linga sarira.* Again, in the so-called " astral body," the fourth principle, when separated from the fifth soon disintegrates, and the so-called fourth principle is almost lifeless unless combined with the fifth. This system of division does not give us any distinct principles which have something like independent existence. And what is more, this sevenfold classification is almost conspicuous by its absence in many of our Hindu books. At any rate a considerable portion of it is almost unintelligible to Hindu minds ; and so it is better to adopt the time-honored classification of four principles, for the simple reason that it divides man into so many entities as are capable of having separate existences, and that these four principles are associated with four *upadhis** which are further associated in their turn with four distinct states of consciousness. And so for all practical purposes—for the purpose of explaining the doctrines of religious philosophy—I have found it far more convenient to adhere to the fourfold clasification than to adopt the septenary one and multiply principles in a manner more likely to introduce confusion than to throw light upon the subject. I shall therefore adopt the four-fold classification, and when I adopt it in the case of man, I shall also adopt it

* Four Upadhis including the Ego—the reflected image of the Logos in Karana Sarira—as the vehicle of the Light of the Logos. This is sometimes called Samanya Sarira in Hindu books. But strictly speaking there are only three Upadhis.

in the case of the solar system, and also in the case of the principles that are to be found in the cosmos. By cosmos I mean not the solar system only, but the whole of the cosmos.

In enumerating these principles I shall proceed in the order of evolution, which seems to be the most convenient one.

I shall point out what position each of these principles occupies in the evolution of nature, and in passing from the First Cause to the organized human being of the present day, I shall give you the basis of the fourfold classification that I have promised to adopt.

The first principle, or rather the first postulate, which I have to lay down is the existence of what is called *Parabrahmam.* Of course there is hardly a system of philosophy which has ever denied the existence of the First Cause. Even the so-called atheists have never denied it. Various creeds have adopted various theories as to the nature of this First Cause. All sectarian disputes and differences have arisen, not from a difference of opinion as to the existence of the First Cause, but from the difference of the attributes that man's intellect has constantly tried to impose upon it. Is it possible to know anything of the First Cause? No doubt it is possible to know something about it. It is possible to know all about its manifestations, though it is next to impossible for human knowledge to penetrate into its inmost essence and say what it really is in itself. All religious philosophers are agreed that this First Cause is omnipresent and eternal. Further, it is subject to periods of activity and passivity. When *cosmic pralaya* comes, it is inactive, and when evolution commences, it becomes active.

But even the real reason for this activity and passivity is unintelligible to our minds. It is not matter or anything like matter. It is not even consciousness, because all that we know of consciousness is with reference to a definite organism. What consciousness is or will be when entirely separated from *upadhi* is a thing utterly inconceivable to us, not only to us but to any other intelligence which has the notion of self or ego in it, or which has a distinct individualized existence. Again it is not even *atma.* The word *atma* is used in various senses in our books. It is constantly associated with the idea of self. But *Parabrahmam* is not so associated ; so it is not ego, it is not non-ego, nor is it consciousness—or to use a phraseology adopted by our old philosophers, it is not *gñatha,* not *gñanam* and *gñayam.* Of course every entity in this cosmos must come under one or the other of these three headings. But *Parabrahmam* does not come under any one of them. Nevertheless, it seems to be the one source of which *gñatha, gñanam, and gñayam* are the manifestations or modes of existence. There are a few other aspects which it is necessary for me to bring to your notice, because those aspects are noticed in the Bhagavad Gita.

In the case of every objective consciousness, we know that what we call matter or non-ego is, after all, a mere bundle of attributes. But whether we arrive at our conclusion by logical inference, or whether we derive it from innate consciousness, we always suppose that there is an entity,—the real essence of the thing upon which all these attributes are placed,—which bears these attributes, as it were, the essence itself being unknown to us.

All Vedantic writers of old have formulated the principle that *Parabrahmam* is the one essence of everything in the cosmos. When our old writers said "*Sarvam khalvidambrahma,*" they did not mean that all those attributes which we associate with the idea of non-ego should be considered as Brahmam, nor did they mean that Brahmam should be looked upon as the *upadana karanam* in the same way that earth and water are the *upadana karanam* of this pillar. They simply meant that the real thing in the bundle of attributes that our consciousness takes note of, the essence which seems to be the bottom and the foundation of all phenomena is *Parabrahmam,* which, though not itself an object of knowledge, is yet capable of supporting and giving rise to every kind of object and every kind of existence which becomes an object of knowledge.

Now this *Parabrahmam* which exists before all things in the cosmos is the one essence from which starts into existence a centre of energy, which I shall for the present call the *Logos.*

This *Logos* may be called in the language of old writers either *Eswara* or *Pratyagatma* or *Sabda Brahmam.* It is called the *Verbum* or the Word by the Christians, and it is the divine *Christos* who is eternally in the bosom of his father. It is called *Avalokiteswara* by the Buddhists ; at any rate, *Avalokiteswara* in one sense is the *Logos* in general, though no doubt in the Chinese doctrine there are also other ideas with which it is associated. In almost every doctrine they have formulated the existence of a centre of spiritual energy which is unborn and eternal, and which exists in a latent condition in the bosom of *Parabrahmam* at the time of *pralaya,* and starts as a centre of conscious energy at the time of cosmic activity. It is the first *gñatha* or the ego in the cosmos, and every other ego and every other self, as I shall hereafter point out, is but its reflection or manifestation. In its inmost nature it is not *unknowable* as *Parabrahmam,* but it is an object of the highest knowledge that man is capable of acquiring. It is the one great mystery in the cosmos, with reference to which all the initiations and all the systems of philosophy have been devised. What it really is in its inmost nature will not be a subject for consideration in my lecture, but there are some stand-points from which we have to look at it to understand the teachings in the Bhagavad Gita.

The few propositions that I am going to lay down with reference to this principle are these. It is not material or physical in its constitution, and it is not objective; it is not different in substance, as it were, or in essence, from *Parabrahmam*, and yet at the same time it is different from it in having an individualized existence. It exists in a latent condition in the bosom of *Parabrahmam*, at the time of pralaya just, for instance, as the sense of ego is latent at the time of *sushupti* or sleep. It is often described in our books as *satchidanandam*, and by this epithet you must understand that it is *sat*, and that it is *chit* and *anandam*.

It has consciousness and an individuality of its own. I may as well say that it is the only *personal* God, perhaps, that exists in the cosmos. But not to cause any misunderstanding I must also state that such centres of energy are almost innumerable in the bosom of *Parabrahmam*. It must not be supposed that this *Logos* is but a single centre of energy which is manifested by *Parabrahmam*. There are innumerable others. Their number is almost infinite. Perhaps even in this centre of energy called the *Logos* there may be differences; that is to say, *Parabrahmam* can manifest itself as a *Logos* not only in one particular, definite, form, but in various forms. At any rate, whatever may be the variations of form that may exist, it is unnecessary to go minutely into that subject for the purpose of understanding the Bhagavad Gita. The *Logos* is here considered the *Logos* in the abstract and not as any particular *Logos*, in giving all those instructions to Arjuna which are of a general application. The other aspect of the *Logos* will be better understood if I point out to you the nature of the other principles that start into existence subsequent to the existence of this *Logos* or *Verbum*.

Of course, this is the first manifestation of *Parabrahmam*, the first ego that appears in the cosmos, the beginning of all creation and the end of all evolution. It is the one source of all energy in the cosmos, and the basis of all branches of knowledge and what is more, it is, as it were, the tree of life, because the *chaitanyam* which animates the whole cosmos springs from it. When once this ego starts into existence as a conscious being having objective consciousness of its own, we shall have to see what the result of this objective consciousness will be with reference to the one absolute and unconditioned existence from which it starts into manifested existence. From its objective standpoint, *Parabrahmam* appears to it as *Mulaprakriti.* Please bear this in mind and try to understand my words, for here is the root of the whole difficulty about *Purusha* and *Prakriti* felt by the various writers on Vedantic philosophy. Of course, this *Mulaprakriti* is material to us. This *Mulaprakriti* is no more *Parabrahmam* than the bundle of attributes of this pillar is the pillar itself ; *Parabrahmam* is an unconditioned and absolute reality, and *Mulaprakriti* is a sort of veil thrown over it. *Parabrahmam* by itself cannot be seen as it is. It is seen by the *Logos* with a veil thrown over it, and that veil is the mighty expanse of cosmic matter. It is the basis of material manifestations in the cosmos.

Again, *Parabrahmam,* after having appeared on the one hand as the ego, and on the other as *Mulaprakriti,* acts as the one energy through the *Logos.* I shall explain to you what I mean by this acting through the *Logos* by a simile. Of course you must not stretch it very far ; it is intended simply to help you to form some kind of conception of the *Logos.* For instance, the sun may be compared with the *Logos* ; light and heat radiate from it, but its heat and energy exist in some unknown condition in space, and are diffused throughout space as visible light and heat through its instrumentality. Such is the view taken of the sun by the ancient philosophers. In the same manner *Parabrahmam* radiates from the *Logos,* and manifests itself as the light and energy of the *Logos*. Now we see the first manifestation of *Parabrahmam* is a Trinity , the highest Trinity that we are capable of understanding. It consists of *Mulaprakriti*, *Esawara* or the *Logos*, and the conscious energy of the *Logos*, which is its power and light; and here we have the three principles upon which the whole cosmos seems to be based. First, we have matter ; secondly, we have force—at any rate, the foundation of all the forces in the cosmos ; and thirdly, we have the ego or the one root of self, of which every other kind of self is but a manifestation or a reflection. You must bear in mind that there is a clear line of distinction drawn between *Mulaprakriti*, (which is, as it were, the veil thrown over *Parabrahmam* from the objective point of view of the *Logos*) and this energy which is radiated from it. Krishna, in the Bhagavad Gita, as I shall hereafter point out, draws a clear line of distinction between the two ; and the importance of the distinction will be seen when you take note of the various misconceptions to which a confusion of the two has given rise in various systems of philosophy. Now bear in mind that this *Mulaprakriti* which is the veil of *Parabrahmam* is called *Avyaktam* in Sankhya philosophy. It is also called *Kutastha* in the Bhagavad Gita, simply because it is undifferentiated ; even the literal meaning of this word conveys more or less the idea that it is undifferentiated as contrasted with differentiated matter. This light from the *Logos* is called *Daiviprakriti* in the Bhagavad Gita ; it is the Gnostic *Sophia* and the Holy Ghost of the Christians. It is a mistake to suppose that Krishna, when considered as a *Logos*, is a manifestation of that *Avyaktam*, as is generally believed by a certain school of philosophers. He is on the other hand *Parabrahmam* manifested ; and the Holy Ghost in its first origin emanates through the *Christos*. The reason why it is called the mother of the *Christos* is this.

When *Christos* manifests himself in man as his Saviour it is from the womb, as it were, of this divine light that he is born. So it is only when the *Logos* is manifested in man that he becomes the child of this light of the *Logos*—this *maya*—but in the course of cosmic manifestation this *Daiviprakriti,* instead of being the mother of the *Logos*, should, strictly speaking, be called the daughter of the *Logos.* To make this clearer, I may point out that this light is symbolized as *Gayatri.* You know *Gayatri* is not *Prakriti.* It is considered as the light of the *Logos*, and in order to convey to our minds a definite image, it is represented as the light of the sun. But the sun from which it springs is not the physical sun that we see, but the central sun of the light of wisdom. This light is further called the *maha-chaitanyam* of the whôle cosmos. It is the life of the whole of nature. It will be observed that what manifests itself as light, as consciousness, and as force, is just one and the same energy. All the various kinds of forces that we know of, all the various modes of consciousness with which we are acquainted, and life manifested in every kind of organism, are but the manifestations of one and the same power, that power being the one that springs from the *Logos* originally. It will have to be surveyed in all these aspects, because the part that it really plays in the cosmos is one of considerable importance.

As far as we have gone we have arrived at firstly, *Parabrahmam*; secondly, *Eswara*; thirdly, the light manifested through *Eswara*, which is called *Daiviprakrati* in the Bhagavad Gita, and lastly that *Mulaprakriti* which seems to be, as I have said, a veil thrown over *Parabrahmam.* Now creation or evolution is commenced by the intellectual energy of the *Logos.* The universe in its infinite details and with its wonderful laws, does not spring into existence by mere chance, nor does it spring into existence merely on account of the potentialities locked up in

Mulaprakriti. It comes into existence mainly through the instrumentality of the one source of energy and power existing in the cosmos, which we have named the *Logos*, and which is the one existing representative of the power and wisdom of *Parabrahmam.* Matter acquires all its attributes and all its powers which, in course of time, give such wonderful results in the course of evolution, by the action of this light that emanates from the *Logos* upon *Mulaprakriti.* From our standpoint, it will be very difficult to conceive what kind of matter that may be which has none of those tendencies which are commonly associated with all kinds of matter, and which only acquires all the various properties manifested by it on receiving, as it were this light and energy from the *Logos.* This light of the *Logos* is the link, so to speak, between objective matter and the subjective thought of *Eswara.* It is called in several Buddhist books *fohat.* It is the one instrument with which the *Logos* works.

What springs up in the *Logos* at first is simply an image, a conception of what it is to be in the cosmos. This light or energy catches the image and impresses it upon the cosmic matter which is already manifested. Thus spring into existence all the manifested solar systems. Of course the four principles we have enumerated are eternal, and are common to the whole cosmos. There is not a place in the whole cosmos where these four energies are absent; and these are the elements of the fourfold classification that I have adopted in dealing with the principles of the mighty cosmos itself.

Conceive this manifested solar system in all its principles and in its totality to constitute the *sthula sarira* of the whole cosmos. Look on this light which emanates from the *Logos* as corresponding to the *sukshma sarira* of the cosmos. Conceive further that this *Logos* which is the one germ from which the whole cosmos springs,—which contains the image of the universe,—stands in the position of the *karana sarira* of the cosmos, existing as it does before the cosmos comes into existence. And lastly, conceive that *Parabrahmam* bears the same relation to the *Logos* as our *atma* does to our *karana sarira.*

These, it must be remembered, are the four general principles of the infinite cosmos, not of the solar system. These principles must not be confounded with those enumerated in dealing with the meaning of *Pranava* in Vedantic Philosophy and the Upanishads. In one sense *Pranava* represents the macrocosm and in another sense the microcosm. From one point of view *Pranava* is also intended to mean the infinite cosmos itself, but it is not in that light that it is generally explained in our Vedantic books, and it will not be necessary for me to explain this aspect of *Pranava.* With reference to this subject I may however allude to one other point, which explains the reason why *Eswara* is called *Verbum* or *Logos* ; why in fact it iscalled *Sabda Brahmam.* The explanation I am going to give you will appear thoroughly mystical. But, if mystical, it has a tremendous significance when properly understood. Our old writers said that *Vach* is of four kinds. These are called *para, pasyanti, madhyama, vaikhari.* This statement you will find in the Rig Veda itself and in several of the *Upanishads. Vaikhari Vach* is what we utter. Every kind of *Vaikhari Vach* exists in its *madhyama,* further in its *pasyanti,* and ultimately in its *para* form. The reason why this *Pranava* is called *Vach* is this, that these four principles of the great cosmos correspond to these four forms of *Vach.* Now the whole manifested solar system exists in its *sukshma* form in this light or energy of the *Logos,* because its image is caught up and transferred to cosmic matter, and again the whole cosmos must necessarily exist in the one source of energy from which this light emanates. The whole cosmos in its objective form is *vaikhari Vach*, the light of the *Logos* is the *madhyama* form, and the *Logos* itself the *pasyanti* form, and *Parabrahmam* the *para* aspect of that *Vach*. It is by the light of this explanation that we must try to understand certain statements made by various philosophers to the effect that the manifested cosmos is the *Verbum* manifested as cosmos.

These four principles bear the same relationship to one another as do these four conditions or manifestations of *Vach*.

I shall now proceed to an examination of the principles that constitute the solar system itself. Here I find it useful to refer to the explanations generally given with reference to *Pranava* and the meaning of its *matras*. *Pranava* is intended to represent man and also the manifested cosmos, the four principles in the one corresponding to the four in the other. The four principles in the manifested cosmos may be enumerated in this order. First, *Vishwanara*. Now this *Vishwanara* is not to be looked upon as merely the manifested objective world, but as the one physical basis from which the whole objective world started into existence. Beyond this, and next to this, is what is called *Hiranyagarbha*. This again is not to be confounded with the astral world, but must be looked upon as the basis of the astral world, bearing the same relationship to the astral world as *Vishwanara* bears to the objective world. Next to this there is what is now and then called *Eswara*; but as this word is likely to mislead, I shall not call it *Eswara*, but by another name, also sanctioned by usage—*Sutratma*. And beyond these three it is generally stated there is *Parabrahmam*. As regards this fourth principle differences of opinion have sprung up, and from these differences any amount of difficulty has arisen. For this principle, we ought to have, as we have for the cosmos, some principle or entity out of which the other three principles start into existence and which exist in it and by reason of it. If such be the case, no doubt we ought to accept the *Avyaktam* of the Sankhyas as this fourth principle. This *Avyaktam* is the *Mulaprakriti* which I have already explained as the *veil* of *Parabrahmam* considered from the objective standpoint of the *Logos*, and this is the view adopted by the majority of the Sankhyas. Into the details of the evolution of the solar system itself, it is not necessary for me to enter. You may gather some idea as to the way in which the various elements start into existence from these three principles into which *Mulaprakriti* is differentiated, by examining the lecture delivered by Professor Crookes a short time ago upon the so-called elements of modern chemistry. This lecture will at least give you some idea of the way in which the so-called elements spring from *Vishwanara* the most objective of these three principles, which seem to stand in the place of the *protyle* mentioned in that lecture. Except in a few particulars, this lecture seems to give the outlines of the theory of physical evolution on the plane of *Vishwanara* and is, as far as I know, the nearest approach made by modern investigators to the real occult theory on the subject.

These principles, in themselves, are so far beyond our common experience as to become objects of merely theoretical conception and inference rather than objects of practical knowledge. Of course if it is so difficult for us to understand these different principles as they exist in nature, it will be still more difficult for us to form any definite idea as to their basis. But at any rate the evolution and the work of differentiation of these principles is a matter which appertains more properly to the science of physics, than to the science of spiritual ethics, and the fundamental principles that I have laid down will suffice for our present purpose. You must conceive, without my going through the whole process of evolution, that out of these three principles, having as their one foundation *Mulaprakriti* the whole manfested solar system with all the various objects in it has started into being. Bear in mind also that the one energy which works out the whole process of evolution is that light of the *Logos* which is diffused through all these principles and all their manifestations. It is the one light that starts with a certain definite impulse communicated by the intellectual energy of the *Logos* and works out the whole programme from the commencement to the end of evolution. If we begin our examination from the lowest organisms, it will be seen that this one life is, as it were, undifferentiated. Now when we take, for instance, the mineral kingdom, or all those objects in the cosmos which we cannot strictly speaking call living organisms, we find this light undifferentiated. In the course of time when we reach plant life it becomes differentiated to a considerable extent, and organisms are formed which tend more and more towards differentiation And when we reach animal life, we find that the differentiation is more complete, and this light moreover manifests itself as consciousness. It must not be supposed that consciousness is a sort of independent entity created by this light; it is a mode or a manifestation of the light itself, which is life. By the time we reach man, this light becomes differentiated and forms that centre or ego that gives rise to all the mental and physical progress that we see in the process of cosmic evolution. This differentiation results in the first instance from the environment of particular organisms. The various actions evoked in a given organism and those which it evokes in other organisms or in its surroundings, and the actions which it generates in itself at that stage, can hardly be called *Karma*; still its life and actions may perhaps have a certain effect in determining the future manifestations of that life-energy which is acting in it. By the time we reach man, this one light becomes differentiated into certain monads, and hence individuality is fixed.

As individuality is rendered more and more definite, and becomes more and more differentiated from other individualities by man's own surroundings, and the intellectual and moral impulses he generates and the effect of his own *Karma*, the principles of which he is composed become more defined. There are four principles in man. First, there is the physical body, about which we need not go into details, as they appertain more to the field of enquiry of the physiologist than to that of the religious investigator. No doubt certain branches of physiology do become matters of considerable importance in dealing with certain subjects connected with Yoga Philosophy; but we need not discuss those questions at present.

Next there is the *sukshma sarira.* This bears to the physical body the same relationship which the astral world bears to the objective plane of the solar system. It is sometimes called *kamarupa* in our theosophical dissertations. This unfortunate expression has given rise also to a misconception that the principle called *kama* represents this astral body itself, and is transformed into it. But it is not so. It is composed of elements of quite a different nature. Its senses are not so differentiated and localized as in the physical body, and, being composed of finer materials, its powers of action and thought are considerably greater than those found in the physical organism. *Karana sarira* can only be conceived as a centre of *pragna*—a centre of force or energy into which the third principle (or *sutratma*) of the cosmos was differentiated by reason of the same impulse which has brought about the differentiation of all these cosmic principles. And now the question is, what is it that completes this trinity and makes it a quaternary?* Of course this light of

* The reflected image of the *Logos* formed by the action of this light or *Karana Sarira* may be considered as the 4th principle in man and it has been so considered by certain philosophers. But in reality the real entity is the light itself and not the reflected image.

the *Logos*. As I have already said, it is a sort of light that permeates every kind of organism, and so in this trinity it is manifested in every one of the *upadhis* as the real *jiva* or the ego of man. Now in order to enable you to have a clear conception of the matter, I shall express my ideas in figurative language. Suppose, for instance, we compare the *Logos* itself to the sun. Suppose I take a clear mirror in my hand, catch a reflection of the sun, make the rays reflect from the surface of the mirror—say upon a polished metallic plate—and make the rays which are reflected in their turn from the plate fall upon a wall. Now we have three images, one being clearer than the other, and one being more resplendent than the other. I can compare the clear mirror to *karana sarira*, the metallic plate to the astral body, and the wall to the physical body. In each case a definite *bimbam* is formed, and that *bimbam* or reflected image is for the time being considered as the self. The *bimbam* formed on the astral body gives rise to the idea of self in it when considered apart from the physical body; the *bimbam* formed in the *karana sarira* gives rise to the most prominent form of individuality that man possesses. You will further see that these various *bimbams* are not of the same lustre. The lustre of this *bimbam* you may compare to man's knowledge, and it grows feebler and feebler as the reflection is transferred from a clear *upadhi* to one less clear, and so on till you get to the physical body. Our knowledge depends mainly on the condition of the *upadhi*, and you will also observe that just as the image of the sun on a clear surface of water may be disturbed and rendered invisible by the motion of the water itself, so by a man's passions and emotions he may render the image of his true self disturbed and distorted in its appearance, and even make the image so indistinct as to be altogether unable to perceive its light.

You will further see that this idea of self is a delusive one. Almost every great writer on Vedantic philosophy, as also both Buddha aud Sankaracharya, have distinctly alleged that it is a delusive idea. You must not suppose that these great men said that the idea of self was delusive for the same reason which led John Stuart Mill to suppose that the idea of self is manufactured from a concatenation or series of mental states. It is not a manufactured idea, as it were, not a secondary idea which has arisen from any series of mental states. It is said to be delusive, as I have been trying to explain, because the real self is the *Logos* itself, and what is generally considered as the ego is but its reflection. If you say, however, that a reflected image cannot act as an individual being, I have simply to remind you that my simile cannot be carried very far. We find that each distinct image can form a separate centre. You will see in what difficulty it will land us if you deny this, and hold the self to be a separate entity in itself. If so, while I am in my objective state of consciousness, my ego is something existing as a real entity in the physical body itself. How is it possible to transfer the same to the astral body? Then, again, it has also to be transferred to the *karana sarira*. We shall find a still greater difficulty in transferring this entity to the *Logos* itself, and you may depend upon it that unless a man's individuality or ego can be transferred to the *Logos* immortality is only a name. In certain peculiar cases it will be very difficult to account for a large number of phenomena on the basis that this self is some kind of centre of energy or some existing monad transferred from *upadhi* to *upadhi*.

In the opinion of the Vedantists, and, as I shall hereafter point out, in the opinion of Krishna also, man is a quaternary. He has first the physical body or *sthula sarira*, secondly the astral body or *sukshma sarira*, thirdly the seat of his higher individuality, the *karana sarira,* and fourthly and lastly, his *atma.* There is no doubt a difference of opinion as to the exact nature of the fourth principle as I have already said, which has given rise to various misconceptions. Now, for instance, according to some followers of the Sankhya philosophy, at any rate those who are called *nireswara sankhyas*, man has these three principles, with their *Avyaktam* to complete the quaternary. This *Avyaktam* is *Mulaprakriti* or rather *Parabrahmam* manifested in *Mulaprakriti* as its *upadhi.* In this view *Parabrahmam* is really the fourth principle, the highest principle in man ; and the other three principles simply exist in it and by reason of it. That is to say, this *Avyaktam* is the one principle which is the root of all self, which becomes differentiated in the course of evolution, or rather which appears to be differentiated in the various organisms, which subsists in every kind of *upadhi* and which is the real spiritual entity which a man has to reach.

Now let us see what will happen accordiug to this hypothesis The *Logos* is entirely shut out ; it is not taken notice of at all; and that is the reason why these people have been called *nireswara sankhyas* (not because they have denied the existence of *Parabrahmam* for this they did not—but) because they have not taken notice of the *Logos*, and its light—the two most important entities in nature,—in classifying the principles of man.

II.

In my last lecture I tried to trace the course of the first beginnings of cosmic evolution, and in doing so I indicated with a certain amount of definiteness the four main principles that operate in the infinite cosmos. I also enumerated the four principles that seemed to form the basis of the whole manifested solar system, and defined the nature of the four principles into which I have divided the constitution of man. I hope that you will bear in mind the explanations that I have given, because it is on a clear understanding of these principles that the whole Vedantic doctrine is explicable; and, moreover, on account of misconceptions introduced as regards the nature of these principles, the religious philosophies of various nations have become terribly confused, and inferences have been drawn from wrong assumptions, which would not necessarily follow from a correct understanding of these principles.

In order to make my position clear, I have yet to make a few more remarks about some of these principles. You will remember that I have divided the solar system itself into four main principles and called them by the names assigned to them in treatises on what may be called *Tharaka Yoga*. *Tharam*, or *Pranava* is also the symbol of the manifested man. And the three *Matras* without the *Ardhamatra* symbolize the three principles, or the three manifestations of the original *Mulaprakriti* in the solar system. *Sankhya Yoga*, properly so called mainly deals with these three principles and the evolution from them of all material organisms. I use the word material to indicate, not only the physical and astral organisms, but also organisms on the plane higher than the astral. Much of what lies on this plane also is in my opinion physical, though perhaps it may differ in its constitution from the known forms of matter on the ordinary objective plane. The whole of this manifested solar system is, strictly speaking, within the field of physical research. As yet we have only been surveying the superficies of the outward cosmos. It is that, and that alone, which physical science has, up to this time, reached. I have not the slightest doubt that in course of time physical science will be able to penetrate deep into the underlying basis, that corresponds to the *Sutratma* of our Vedantic writers.

It is the province of Sankhya philosophy to trace from the three component parts of *Mulaprakriti* all the various physical manifestations. It must not, however, be supposed that I in any way authorize the way in which Sankhya philosophy, as at present understood, traces out the origin of these manifestations. On the contrary, there is every reason to believe that enquirers into physical science in the West, like Professor Crookes and others, will arrive at truer results than are contained in the existing systems of Sankhya philosophy known to the public. Occult science has, of course, a definite theory of its own to propound for the origin of these organisms, but that is a matter that has always been kept in the background, and the details of that theory are not necessary for the purpose of explaining the doctrine of the Bhagavad Gita. It will be sufficient for the present to note what the field of Sankhya philosophy is, and what it is that comes within the horizon of physical science.

We can form no idea as to the kind of beings that exist on the astral plane, and still less are we able to do so in the case of those beings that live on the plane anterior to the astral. To the modern mind, everything else, beyond and beside this ordinary plane of existence, is a perfect blank. But occult science does definitely formulate the existence of these finer planes of being, and the phenomena that now manifest themselves in the so-called spiritualistic seances will give us some idea of the beings living on the astral plane. It is well known that in most of our *Puranas Devas* are mentioned as existing in *Swarga.*

All the *Devaganams* mentioned in the *Puranas* are not in *Swarga. Vasus, Rudras, Adityas* and some other classes are no doubt *Devas* strictly so-called. But *Yakshas, Gandharvas, Kinnaras* and several other *Ganams* must he included amongst the beings that exist in the plane of the astral light.

These beings that inhabit the astral plane are called by the general name of elementals in our theosophical writings. But besides elementals, properly so-called, there are still higher beings, and it is to these latter that the name *Deva* is strictly applicable. Do not make the mistake of thinking that the word *Deva* means a god, and that because we have thirty-three crores of *Devas*, we therefore worship thirty-three crores of gods. This is an unfortunate blunder generally committed by Europeans. *Deva* is a kind of spiritual being, and because the same word is used in ordinary parlance to mean god, it by no means follows that we have and worship thirty-three crores of gods. These beings, as may be naturally inferred, have a certain affinity with one of the three component *upadhis* into which we have divided man.

One organism has always a certain affinity with another organism composed of the same materials and existing on the same plane. As may naturally be expected, the astral body of man has affinity with the elementals, and the so-called *kàrana sarira* of man with the *Devas*. The ancient writers on Hindu philosophy have divided the cosmos into three *lokas*. The first is *Bhuloka*, the second *Bhuvarloka*, and the third *Suvarloka*. *Bhuloka* is the physical plane with which we are generally acquainted. *Bhuvarloka* is, strictly speaking, the astral plane It is sometimes called *Antariksham* in the Upanishads. But this term is not to be understood as simply meaning the whole extent of the atmosphere with which we are acquainted. The word *Antariksham* is used, not in its general sense, but in a technical one belonging to the philosophical terminology adopted by the authors of the works in which it occurs. *Suvarloka* is what is generally known as *Swargam*. At any rate it is the *Devachan* of the theosophical writings. In this place, called *Devachan* by the Buddhists, and *Swargam* by the Hindus, we locate the higher orders of the so-called *Devaganams*.

There is one more statement I have to make with reference to the three *Upadhis* in the human being. Of these what is called the *karana sarira* is the most important. It is so, because it is in that that the higher individuality of man exists. Birth after birth a new physical body comes into existence, and perishes when earthly life is over. The astral body, when once separated from the *karana sarira* may perhaps live on for some time, owing to the impulse of action and existence, already communicated to it during life, but, as these influences are cut off from the source whence they originally sprung, the force communicated, as it were, stands by itself, and sooner or later the astral organism becomes completely dissolved into its component parts. But *karana sarira* is a body or organism, which is capable of existing independently of the astral body. Its plane of existence is called *Sutratma,* because, like so many beads strung on a thread, successive personalities are strung on this *karana sarira,* as the individual passes through incarnation after incarnation. By personality I mean that persistent idea of self, with its definite associations, so far as those associations appertain to the experiences of one earthly incarnation.

Of course all the associations or ideas of mental states which a human being may experience are not necessarily communicated to the astral man, much less to the *karana sarira.* Of all the experiences of the physical man, the astral man, or the *karana sarira* beyond it, can only assimilate those whose constitution and nature are similar to its own. It is moreover but consistent with justice that all our mental states should not be preserved as most of them are concerned merely with the daily avocations, or even the physical wants of the human being, there is no object to be gained by their continued preservation. But all that goes deep into the intellectual nature of man, all the higher emotions of the human soul and the intellectual tastes generated in man with all his higher aspirations, do become impressed almost indelibly on the *karana sarira.* The astral body is simply the seat of the lower nature of man. His animal passions and emotions, and those ordinary thoughts which are generally connected with the physical wants of man, may no doubt communicate themselves to the astral man, but higher than this they do not go.

This *karana sarira* is what passes as the real ego, which subsists through incarnation after incarnation, adding in each incarnation something to its fund of experiences, and evolving a higher individuality as the resultant of the whole process of assimilation. It is for this reason that the *karana sarira* is called the ego of man, and in certain systems of philosophy it is called the *jiva.*

It must be clearly borne in mind that this *karana sarira* is primarily the result of the action of the light of the *Logos*, which is its life and energy, and which is further its source of consciousness on that plane of *Mulaprakriti* which we have called *Sutratma,* and which is its physical or material basis.

Out of the combination of these two elements, and from the action of the energy of the light emanating from the *Logos* upon that particular kind of matter that constitutes its physical frame, a kind of individuality is evolved.

I have already said that individual existence, or differentiated conscious existence, is evolved out of the one current of life, which sets the evolutionary machine in motion. I pointed out that it is this very current of life gradually gives rise to individual organisms as it proceeds on its mission. Furthermore it begins to manifest what we call conscious life, and, when we come to man, we find that his conscious individuality is clearly and, completely defined by the operation of this force. In producing this result several subsidiary forces, which are generated by the peculiar conditions of time, space and environment, co-operate with this one life. What is generally called *karana sarira* is but the natural product of the action of those very forces that have operated to bring about this result. When once that plane of consciousness is reached in the path of progress that includes the voluntary actions of man, it will be seen that those voluntary actions not only preserve the individuality of the *karana sarira* but render it more and more definite, as birth after birth further progress is attained and thus keep up the continued existence of the *jiva* as an individual monad. So in one sense the *karana sarira* is the result of karmic impulses. It is the child of *Karma* as it were. It lives with it, and will disappear if the infleunce of *Karma* can be annihilated. The astral body on the other hand is, to a great extent, the result of the physical existence of man, as far as that existence is concerned with his physical wants, associations and cravings. We may therefore suppose that the persistence of astral body after death, will under ordinary circumstances, be more or less proportionate to the strength of these emotions and animal passions.

Now let us enquire what, constituted as man is, are the rules to which he is generally subject, and the goal towards which all evolution is progressing. It is only after this has been determined, that we shall be in a position to see whether any special rules can be prescribed for his guidance that are likely to render his evolutionary progress more rapid than it would otherwise be.

What happens in the case of ordinary men after death is this. First, the *karana sarira* and the astral body separate themselves from the physical body; when that takes place, the physical body loses its life and energy. Yesterday I tried to explain the connection between the three bodies and the energy of life acting within them, by comparing the action of this life to the action of a sunbeam falling successively on three material objects. It will be seen from this comparison, that the light reflected on to the astral body, or rather into the astral body, is the light that radiates from the *karana sarira.* From the astral body it is again reflected on to the *sthula sarira*, constitues its life and energy, and developes that sense of ego that we experience in the physical body. Now it is plain that, if the *karana sarira* is removed, the astral body ceases to receive any reflection. The *karana sarira* can exist independently of the astral body, but the astral body cannot survive the separation of the *karana sarira.* Similarly the physical body can go on living so long as it is connected with the astral body and the *karana sarira;* but, when these two are removed, the physical body will perish. The only way for the life current to pass to the physical body is through the medium of the astral body. The physical body is dissolved when separated from the astral body because the impulse that animated it is removed. As the *karana sarira* is on the plane of *Devachan*, the only place to which it can go on separation from the physical body is *Devachan*, or *Swargam* ; but in separating itself from the astral body it takes with it all those impulses, that were accumulated by the karma of the man during his successive incarnations.

These impulses subsist in it, and perhaps it does enjoy a new life in *Devachan*—a life unlike any with which we are acquainted, but a life quite as natural to the entity that enjoys it as our conscious existence seems to be to us now These impulses give rise to a further incarnation, because there is a certain amount of energy locked up in them, which must find its manifestation on the physical plane. It is thus karma that leads it on from incarnation to incarnation.

The natural region of the astral body is the *Bhuvarloka* or astral plane. To the astral plane it goes, and there it is detained. It very rarely descends into the physical plane, for the simple reason that the physical plane has no natural attraction for it. Moreover it necessarily follows that, just as the *karana sarira* cannot remain on the physical plane, the astral body cannot remain there either. This astral body loses its life impulse when the *karana sarira* is separated from it. When once its source of life and energy is thus removed from it, it is naturally deprived of the only spring of life that can enable it to subsist. But astral matter being of a far finer constitution than physical matter, energy once communicated to it subsists for a longer time than when communicated to physical matter. When once separated from the astral body, the physical body dies very rapidly, but in the case of the astral body some time is required before complete dissolutiou can take place, because the impulses already communicated to it still keep the particles together, and its period of post-mortem existence is proportionate to the strength of those impulses. Till this strength is exhausted the astral body holds together. The time of its independent existence on the astral plane will thus depend on the strength of its craving for life and the intensity of its unsatisfied desires. This is the reason why, in the case of suicides and those who die premature deaths, having at the time of death a strong passion or a strong desire that they were unable to satisfy during life, but on the fulfilment of which their whole energy was concentrated, the astral body subsists for certain length of time, and may even make desperate efforts for the purpose of descending into the physical plane to bring about the accomplishment of its object. Most of the spirtualistic phenomena are to be accounted for upon this principle, and also upon the principle that many of the phenomena exhibited at seances are really produced by elementals (which naturally subsist on the astral plane) masquerading as it were in the garb of elementaries or *pisachas*.

I need not, however, enter further into this branch of the subject, as it has but a very remote bearing upon the teachings of the Bhagavad Gita with which I am concerned. Suffice it to say, that what has been stated is all that ordinarily takes place at the death of a man, but there are certain kinds of karma which may present exceptions to the general law. Suppose, for instance, a man has devoted all his life to the evocation of elementals. In such a case either the elementals take possession of the man and make a medium of him, or, if they do not do that completely, they take possession of his astral body and absorb it at the time of death. In the latter case the astral body, associated as it is with an independent elemental being, will subsist for a considerable length of time. But though elemental worship may lead to mediumship—to irresponsible mediumship in the majority of cases—and may confuse a man's intellect, and make him morally worse than he was before, these elementals will not be able to destroy the *karana sarira.* Still it is by no means a desirable thing, that we should place ourselves under the control of elementals.

There is another kind of worship, however, which a man may follow, and which may lead to far more serious results. What may happen to the astral body, may also happen to the *karana sarira.* The *karana sarira* bears the same relation to the *Devas* in *Swargam* that the astral body does to the elementals on the astral plane. In this *Devaloka* there are beings, or entities, some vicious and some good, and, if a man who wishes to evoke these powers were to fix his attention upon them, he might in course of time attract these powers to himself, and it is quite possible that when the force generated by the concentration of his attention upon these beings attains a certain amount of strength, the *karana sarira* may be absorbed into one of these *Devas*, just as the astral body may be absorbed into an elemental.

This is a far more serious result than any that can happen to man in the case of elemental worship, for the simple reason that he has no more prospect of reaching the *Logos*.

The whole of his individuality is absorbed into one of these beings, and it will subsist as long as that being exists, and no longer. When cosmic *pralaya* comes it will be dissolved, as all these beings will be dissolved. For him there is no immortality. He may indeed have life for millions of years, but what are millions of years to immortality? You will recollect that it is said in Mr. Sinnett's book, that there is such a thing as immortality in evil. The statement, as it stands, is no doubt an exaggeration. What Mr. Sinnett meant to say was, that, when those who follow the left-hand path evoke certain powers which are wicked in their nature, they may transfer their own individualities to those powers, and subsist in them until the time of cosmic *pralaya* These would then become formidable powers in the cosmos, and, would interfere to a considerable extent in the affairs of mankind. and even prove far more troublesome, so far as humanity is concerned, than the genuine powers themselves on account of the association of a human individuality with one of these powers. It was for this reason that all great religions have inculcated the great truth, that man should not, for the sake of gain or profit, or for the acquisition of any object, however tempting for the time being, worship any such powers, but should wholly devote his attention and worship to the one true *Logos* accepted by every true and great religion in the world, as that alone can lead a man safely along the true moral path, and enable him to rise higher and higher, until he lives in it as an immortal being, as the manifested *Eswara* of the cosmos, and as the source, if necessary, of spiritual enlightenment to generations to come.

It is towards this end, which may be hastened in certain cases, that all evolution is tending. The one great power, that is as it were guiding the whole course of evolution, leading nature on towards its goal, so to speak, is the light of the *Logos*. The *Logos* is as it were the pattern, and emanating from it is this light of life. It goes forth into the world with this pattern imprinted upon it, and, after going through the whole cycle of evolution, it tries to return to the *Logos* whence it had its rise. Evolutionary progress is effected by the continual perfecting of the *Upadhi*, or organism through which this light works. In itself it has no need of improvement. What is perfected is, neither the *Logos*, nor the light of the *Logos*, but the *Upadhi* or physical frame through which this light is acting. I have already said that it is upon the purity and nature of this *Upadhi*, that the manifested clearness and refulgence of the *Logos* mainly depends. As time goes on, man's intelligence on the spiritual, astral and physical planes will become more and more perfect, as the *Upadhis* are perfected, until a certain point is reached when he will be enabled to make the final attempt to perceive and recognise his *Logos*, unless he chooses to wilfully shut his eyes, and prefers perdition to immortality. It is towards this end that nature is working.

I have pointed out the fact that there are certain cases which may cause a disturbance in the general progress, and I have mentioned the causes that may facilitate that progress. All the initiations that man ever invented were invented for the purpose of giving men a clear idea of the *Logos*, to point out the goal, and to lay down rules by which it is possible to facilitate the approach to the end towards which nature is constantly working.

These are the premises from which Krishna starts. Whethe by express statements, or by necessary implications, all these propositions are present in this book, and, taking his stand on these fundamental propositions, Krishna proceeds to construct his practical theory of life.

In stating this theory I have not made any reference to particular passages in the Bhagavad Gita. By constantly turning to the detached passages in which these propositions are expressed or implied, I should have only created confusion, it therefore seemed better to begin by stating the theory in my own language, in order to give you a connected idea of it as a whole. I do not think it will be allowed by every follower of every religion in India, that these are the propositions from which Krishna started. The theory has been misunderstood by a considerable number of philosphers, and, in course of time, the speculations of the Sankhyas have introduced a source of error, which has exercised a most important influence on the development of Hindu philosophy. There is not however the slightest doubt in my own mind, that what I have said includes the basis of the real Vedantic philosophy. Having but little time at my command I have thought it unnecessary to cite authorities : had I done so it would have taken me not three days, but three years, to explain the philosophy of the Bhagavad Gita. I shall leave it to you to examine these propositions and to carefully ascertain how far they seem to underlie, not merely Hinduism, but Buddhism, the ancient philosophies of the Egyptians and the Chaldeans, the speculations of the Rosicrucians, and almost every other system having the remotest connection with occultism from times long antecedent to the so-called historic periods.

I will now turn to the book itself :

Krishna is generally supposed to be an *Avatar*. This theory of *Avatars* plays a very important part in Hindu philosophy ; and, unless it is properly understood, it is likely that great misconceptions will arise from the acceptance of the current views regarding this *Avatar*. It is generally supposed that Krishna is the *Avatar* of the one great personal God who exists in the cosmos. Of course those who hold this view make no attempt to explain how this one great personal God succeeded in setting up an intimate connection with the physical body of Krishna, constituted as the physical body of every man is, or even with a personality, or human individuality, that seems to be precisely similar to that of any other human being. And how are we to explain the theory of *Avatars*, as generally stated with reference to the view of this particular *Avatar* to which I have referred? This view is without any support. The *Logos* in itself is not the one personal God of the cosmos. The great, *Parabrahmam* behind it is indeed one and *niramsa* undifferentiated and eternally existing, but that *Parabrahmam* can never manifest itself as any of these *Avatars*. It does, of course, manifest itself in a peculiar way as the whole cosmos, or rather as the supposed basin, or the one essence, on which the whole cosmos seems to be superimposed, the one foundation for every existence. But it can manifest itself in a manner approaching the conception of a personal God, only when it manifests itself as the *Logos*. If *Avatars* are possible at all, they can only be so with reference to the *Logos*, or *Eswara*, and not by any means with reference to what I have called *Parabrahmam*. But still there remains the question, what is an *Avatar?* According to the general theory I have laid down, in the case of every man who becomes a *Mukta* there is a union with the *Logos*. It may be conceived, either as the soul being raised to the *Logos*, or as the *Logos* descending from its high plane to associate itself with the soul. In the generality of cases, this association of the soul with the *Logos* is only completed after death—the last death which that individual has to go through.

But in some special cases the *Logos* does descend to the plane of the soul and associate itself with the soul during the life-time of the individual; but these cases are very rare. In the case of such beings, while they still exist as ordinary men on the physical plane, instead of having for their soul merely the reflection of the *Logos*, they have the *Logos* itself. Such beings have appeared. Buddhists say, that in the case of Buddha there was this permanent union, when he attained what they call *Para-nirvana* nearly twenty years before the death of his physical body. Christians say, that the *Logos* was made flesh, as it were, and was born as Christ—as Jesus—though the Christians do not go into a clear analysis of the propositions they lay down. There are, however, certain sections of Christians, who take a more philosophical view of the question, and say that the divine *Logos* associated itself with the man named Jesus at some time during his career, and that it was only after that union he began to perform his miracles and show his power as a great reformer and saviour of mankind.

Whether this union took place as a special case in the case of Jesus, or whether it was such a union as would take place in the case of every Mahatma or Maharishi when he becomes a *Jivanmukta,* we cannot say, unless we know a great deal more about him than what the Bible can teach us. In the case of Krishna the same question arises. Mahavishnu is a God, and is a representative of the *Logos* ; he is considered as the *Logos* by the majority of Hindus. From this it must not however be inferred that there is but one *Logos* in the cosmos, or even that but one form of *Logos* is possible in the cosmos. For the present I am only concerned with this form of the *Logos*, and it seems to be the foundation of the teachings we are considering.

There are two views which you can take with reference to such human *Avatars,* as for instance, Rama, Krishna, and Parasurama. Some Vaishnavites deny that Buddha was an *Avatar* of Vishnu. But that was an exceptional case and is very little understood by either Vaishnavites or Buddhists

Parasurama's *Avatar* will certainly be disputed by some writers. I believe that, looking at the terrible things he did, the Madwas thought that, in the case of Parasurama, there was no real *Avatar*, but a mere over-shadowing of the man by Mahavishnu. But, setting aside disputed cases,we have two. undisputed human *Avatars*—Rama and Krishna.

Take for instance the case of Krishna. In this case two views are possible. We may suppose that Krishna, as an individual, was a man who had been evoluting for millions of years, and had attained great spiritual perfection, and that in the course of his spiritual progress the *Logos* descended to him and associated itself with his soul. In that case it is not the *Logos* that manifested itself as Krishna, but Krishna who raised himself to the position of the *Logos*. In the case of a Mahatma who becomes a *Jivanmukta*, it is his soul, as it were that is transformed into the *Logos*. In the case of a *Logos* descending into a man, it does so, not chiefly by reason of that man's spiritual perfection, but for some ulterior purpose of its own for the benefit of humanity. In this case it is the *Logos* that descends to the plane of the soul and manifests its energy in and though the soul, and not the soul that ascends to the plane of the *Logos*.

Theoretically it is possible for us to entertain either of these two views. But there is one difficulity. If we are at liberty to call that man an *Avatar* who becomes a *Jivanmukta*, we shall be obliged to call Suka, Vasishta, Thurvasa and perhaps the whole number of the Maharishis who have become *Jivanmuktas Avatars* ; but they are not generally called *Avatars*. No doubt some great Rishis are enumerated in the list of *Avatars*, given for instance in Bhagavad, but somehow no clear explanation is given for the fact that the ten *Avatars* ordinarily enumerated are looked upon as *the Avatars* of Mahavishnu, and the others as his manifestations, or beings in whom his light and knowledge were placed for the time being ; or for some reason or other, these others are not supposed to be *Avatars* in the strict sense of the word. But, if these are not *Avatars*, then we shall have to suppose that Krishna and Rama are called *Avatars*, not because we have in them an instance of a soul that had become a *Jivanmukta* and so become associated with *the Logos*, but because the *Logos* descended to the plane of the soul, and, associating itself with the soul, worked in and through it on the plane of humanity for some great thing that had to be done in the world. I believe this latter view will be found to be correct on examination. Our respect for Krishna need not in any way be lessened on that account. The real Krishna is not the man in and through whom the *Logos* appeared, but the *Logos* itself. Perhaps our respect will only be enhanced, when we see that this is the case of the *Logos* descending into a human being for the good of humanity. It is not encumbered with any particular individuality in such a case and has perhaps greater power to exert itself for the purpose, of doing good to humanity—not merely for the purpose of doing good to one man, but for the purpose of saving millions.

There are two dark passages in Mahabharata, which will be found very hard nuts for the advocates of the orthodox theory to crack. To begin with Rama. Suppose Rama was not the individual monad plus the *Logos* but in some unaccountable manner the *Logos* made flesh. Then, when the physical body disappeared there should be nothing remaining but the *Logos*—there should be no individual ego to follow its own course. That seems to be the inevitable result, if we are to accept the orthodox theory. But there is a statement made by Narada in the Lokapala Sabha Varnana, in Mahabharata, in which he says, speaking of the court of Yama, who is one of the *Devas*, that Dasaratha

Rama was one of the individuals present there. Now, if the individual Rama was merely a *Maya*—not in the sense in which every human being is a *Maya*, but in a special sense—there is not the slightest reason why he should subsist after the purpose for which this *Maya* garb was wanted was accomplished. It is stated in Ramayana, that the *Logos* went to its place of abode when Rama died, yet we find in Mahabbharata Dasaratha Rama mentioned together with a number of other kings, as an individual present in *Yamaloka*, which, at the highest, takes us only up to *Devachan*. This assertion becomes perfectly consistent with the theory I have laid down, if that is properly understood. Rama was an individual, constituted like every other man. Probably he had had several incarnations before, and was destined, even after his one great incarnation, to have several subsequent births. When he appeared as Rama *Avatar*, it was not Rama's soul transformed into the *Logos*, or rather Rama himself as *Jivanmukta*, that did all the great deeds narrated in the Ramayana—allegorical as it is,—but it was the *Logos*, or Mahavishnu, that descended to the plane of the soul and associated itself for the time being with a particular soul for the purpose of acting through it. Again, in the case of Krishna there is a similar difficulty to be encountered. Turn for instance to the end of the Mousala Parva in the Mahabharata, where you will find a curious passage. Speaking of Krishna's death, the author says that the soul went to heaven—which corresponds to *Devachan* where it was received with due honors by all the *Devas*. Then it is said, that Narayana departed from that place to his own place, Narayana being the symbol of the *Logos*. Immediately after there follows a stanza describing the existence of Krishna in *Swar-gam*, and further on we find that when Dharmaraja's soul went into *Swargam* he found Krishna there. How are these two statements to be reconciled! Unless we suppose that Narayan, whose energy and wisdom were manifested through the man Krishna, was a separate spiritual power manifesting itself for the time being through this individual, there is no solution of the difficulty. Now, from these two statements we shall not be far wrong in inferring that the *Avatars* we are speaking of, were the manifestations of one and the same power, the *Logos*, which the great Hindu writers of old called Mahavishnu. Who then is this Mahavishnu? Why should this *Logos* in particular, if there are several other *Logos* in the universe, take upon itself the care of humanity, and manifest itself in the form of various *Avatars*; and further, is it possible for every other adept, after he becomes associated with the *Logos*, to descend as an *Avatar* in the same manner for the good of humanity?

A clear discussion of these questions will lead into considerations that go far down into the mysteries of occult science, and to explain which clearly I should have to take into account a number of theories that can only be communicated at the time of initiation. Possibly some light will be thrown upon the subject in the forthcoming "Secret Doctrine" but it would be premature for me to discuss the question at this stage. It will be sufficient for me to say, that this Mahavishnu seems to be the Dhyan Chohan that first appeared on this planet when human evolution commenced during this *Kalpa*, who set the evolutionary progress in motion, and whose duty it is to watch over the interests of mankind until the seven *Manwañtars* through which we are passing, are over.

It may be that this *Logos* itself was associated with a *jivanmukta*, or a great Mahatma of a former *Kalpa*. However that may be, it is a *Logos*, and as such only it is of importance to us at present. Perhaps in former *Kalpas*, of which there have been millions, that *Logos* might have associated itself with a series of Mahatma, and all their individualities might have been subsisting in it; nevertheless it has a distinct individuality of his own, it is *Eswara*, and it is only as a *Logos* in the abstract that we have to consider it from present purpose. This explanation, however, I have thought it necessary to give, for the purpose of enabling you to understand certain statements made by Krishna, which will not become intelligible unless read in connection with what I have said.

III.

In this lecture I shall consider the premises I have laid down with special reference to the various passages in which they seem to be indicated in this book.

It will be remembered that I started with the very first cause, which I called *Parabrahmam*. Any positive definition of this principle is of course impossible, and a negative definition is all that can be attempted from the very nature of the case. It is generally believed, at any rate by a certain class of philosophers, that Krishna himself is *Parabrahmam*—that he is the personal God who is *Parabrahmam*—, but the words used by Krishna in speaking of *Parabrahmam*, and the way in which he deals with the subject, clearly show that he draws a distinction between himself and *Parabrahmam*.

No doubt he is a manifestation of *Parabrahmam*, as every *Logos* is. And *Pratyagatma* is *Parabrahmam* in the sense in which that proposition is laid down by the Adwaitis. This statement is at the bottom of all Adwaiti philosophy, but is very often misunderstood. When Adwaitis say "*Aham eva Parabrahmam*," they do not mean to say that this *ahañkaram* (egotism) is *Parabrahmam*, but that the only true *self* in the cosmos which is the *Logos* or *Pratyagatma*, is a manifestation of *Parabrahmam*.

It will be noticed that when Krishna is speaking of himself he never uses the word *Parabrahmam*, but places himself in the position of *pratyagatma* and it is from this standpoint that we constantly find him speaking. Whenever he speaks of *Pratyagatma*, he speaks of himself, and whenever he speaks of *parabrahmam*, he speaks of it as being something different from himself.

I will now go through all the passages in which reference is made to *Parabrahmam* in this book. The first passage to which I shall call your attention is chapter viii, verse 3:—

"The eternal spirit is the Supreme Brahma. Its condition as *Pratyagatma* is called *Adhyatma*. Action which leads to incarnated existence is denoted by Karma."

Here the only words used to denote *Parabrahmam* are *Aksharam* and *Brahma*. These are the words he generally uses. You will notice that he does not in any place call it *Eswara* or *Maheswara*; he does not even allude to it often as *Atma*. Even the term *Paramatma* he applies to himself, and not to *Parabrahmam*. I believe that the reason for this is that the word *Atma*, strictly speaking, means the same thing as self, that idea of self being in no way connected with *Parabrahmam*. This idea of self first comes into existence with the *Logos*, and not before; hence *Parabrahmam* ought not to be called *Paramatma* or any kind of *Atma*. In one place only Krishna, speaking of *Parabrahmam*, says that it is *his Atma*. Except in that case he nowhere uses the word *Atma* or *Paramatma* in speaking of *Parabrahmam*. Strictly speaking *Parabrahmam* is the very foundation of the highest self. *Paramatma* is however a term also applied to *Parabrahmam* as distinguished from *Pratyagatma*. When thus applied it is used in a strictly technical sense. Whenever the term *Pratyagatma* is used, you will find *Paramatma* used as expressing something distinct from it.

It must not be supposed that either the ego, or any idea of self, can be associated with, or be considered as inherent in *Parabrahmam*. Perhaps it may be said that the idea of self is latent in *Parabrahmam*, as everything is latent in it; and, if on that account you connect the idea of self with *Parabrahmam*, you will be quite justified in applying the term *Paramatma* to *Parabrahmam*. But to avoid confusion it is much better to use our words in a clear sense, and to give to each a distinct connotation about which there can be no dispute. Turn now to chapter viii, verse 11 :—

"I will briefly explain to thee that place (*padam*), which those who know the Vedas describe as indestructible (*aksharam*), which the ascetics, who are free from desire, enter, and which is the desired destination of those who observe Brahmacharyam."

Here we find another word used by Krishna when speaking of *Parabrahmam*. He calls it his *padam—the abode of bliss, or Nirvana*. When he calls *Parabrahmam* his *padam* or abode, he does not mean *vaikuntha loka* or any other kind of *loka*; he speaks of it as his abode, because it is in the bosom of *Parabrahmam* that the *Logos* resides. He refers to *Parabrahmam* as the abode of bliss, wherein resides eternally the *Logos*, manifested or unmanifested. Again turn to chapter viii, verse 21 ;—

" That which is stated to be unmanifested and immutable is spoken of as the highest condition to be reached. That place from which there is no return for those who reach it is my supreme abode."

Here the same kind of language is used, and the reference is to *Parabrahmam*. When any soul is absorbed into the *Logos*, or reaches the *Logos*, it may be said to have reached *Parabrahmam*, which is the centre of the *Logos*; and as the *Logos* resides in the bosom of *Parabrahmam*, when the soul reaches the *Logos* it reaches *Parabrahmam* also.

Here you will notice that he again speaks of *Parabrahmam* as his abode.

Turn now to chapter ix, verses 4, 5 and 6 :—

> "The whole of this Universe is pervaded by me in my unmanifested form (*Avyaktamoorti*). I am thus the support of all the manifested existence, but I am not supported by them." Look at my condition when manifested as *Eswara* (*Logos*) : these phenomenal manifestations are not within me. My *Atma* (however) is the foundation and the origin of manifested beings, though it does not exist in combination with them. Conceive that all the manifested beings are within me, just as the atmosphere spreading every-where is always in space."

In my last lecture I tried to explain the mysterious connection between *Parabrahmam* and *Mulaprakriti*. *Parabrahmam* is never differentiated. What is differentiated is *Mulaprakriti*, which is sometimes called *Avyaktam*, and in other places *Kutastham*, which means simply the undifferentiated Element. Nevertheless *Parabrahmam* seems to be the one foundation for all physical phenomena, or for all phenomena that are generally referred to *Mulaprakriti*. After all, any material object is nothing more than a bundle of attributes to us. Either on account of an innate propensity within us or as a matter of inference, we always suppose that there is a non-ego, which has this bundle of attributes superimposed upon it, and which is the basis of all these attributes. Were it not for this essence, there could be no physical body. But these attributes do not spring from *Parabrahmam* itself, but from *Mulaprakriti* which is its veil, *Mulaprakriti* is the veil of *Parabrahmam*. It is not *Parabrahmam* itself, but merely its appearance. It is purely phenomenal. It is no doubt far more persistent than any other kind of objective existence. Being the first mode or manifestation of the only absolute and unconditioned reality it seems to be the basis of all subsequent manifestations. Speaking of this aspect of *Parabrahmam*, Krishna says that the whole cosmos is pervaded by it, which is his *Avyakta* form.

Thus he speaks of *Parabrahmam* as his *Avyaktamoorti*, because *Parabrahmam* is unknowable, and only becomes knowable when manifesting itself as the *Logos* or *Eswara*. Here he is trying to indicate that *Parabrahmam* is the *Avyaktamoorti* of the *Logos* as it is the *Atma* of the *Logos*, which is everywhere present, since it is the *Atma* of the universe, and which appears differentiated, — when manifested in the shape of the various *Logos* working in the cosmos, though in itself it is undifferentiated—, and which, though the basis of all phenomenal manifestations, does not partake of the *vikarams* of those phenomenal manifestations.

Refer now to chapter xii, verses 13, 14, 15, 16, and 17.*

Here again, in speaking of *Parabrahmam* in verses 15, 16, and 17, Krishna is laying down a proposition which I have already explained at length. I need not now go minutely into the meaning of these verses, for you can very easily ascertain them from the commentaries.

Turn to chapter xiv, verse 27 :--

"I am the image or the seat of the immortal and indestructible Brahmama of eternal law and of undisturbed happiness."

Here Krishna is referring to himself as a manifestation or image of *Parabrahmam*. He says he is the *Pratishta* of *Parabrahmam* ; he does not call himself *Parabrahmam*, but only its image or manifestation.

The only other pssage in which Krishna refers to the same subject is chapter xv, verse 6 :—

"That is my supreme abode *(dhama)*, which neither sun, nor moon, nor fire illumines. Those who enter it do not return."

---

* This and some of the other quotations have been omitted on account of their length.—*Ed*

There again he speaks of *padam* and refers to *Parabrahmam* as his abode. I believe that these are all the statements that refer to *Parabrahmam* in this book, and they are sufficient to indicate its position pretty clearly, and to show the nature of its connection with the *Logos*. I shall now proceed to point out the passages in which reference is made to the *Logos* itself.

Strictly speaking the whole of this book may be called the book of the philosophy of the *Logos*. There is hardly a page which does not directely or indirectly refer to it. There are however a few important and significant passages, to which it is desirable that I should refer you, so that you may see whether what I have said about the nature and functions of the *Logos*, and its connection with humanity and the human soul, is supported by the teachings of this book. Let us turn to chapter iv, and examine the meaning of verses 5 to 11 :—

" O Arjuna, I and thou have passed through many births. I know all of them, but thou dost not know, O harasser of foes.

" Even I,who am unborn, imperishable, the Lord of all beings, controlling my own nature, take birth through the instrumentality of my *maya*.

" O Bharata, whenever there is a decline of *dharma* or righteousness and spread of *adharma* or unrighteousness, I create myself.

" I take birth in every *yuga*, to protect the good, to destroy evil-doers and to re-establish *dharma*.

" O Arjuna, he who understands truly my divine birth and action, abandoning his body, reaches me, and does not come to birth again.

" Many, who are free from passion, fear and anger, devoted to me and full of me, purified by spiritual wisdom, have attained my condition."

This passage refers, of course, not only to the *Logos* in the abstract, but also to Krishna's own incarnations. It will be noticed that he speaks here as if his *Logos* had already associated itself with several personalities, or human indvidualities, in former *yugas* ; and he says that he remembers all that took place in connection with those incarnations. Of course, since there could be no *karmabandham* as far as he was concerned, his *Logos*, when it asociated itself with a human soul, would not lose its own independence of action, as a soul confined by the bonds of matter. And because his intellect and wisdom were in no way clouded by this association with a human soul, he says he can recollect all his previous incarnations, while Arjuna, not yet having fully received the light of the *Logos* is not in a position to understand all that took place in connection with his former births. He says that it is his object to look after the welfare of humanity, and that whenever a special incarnation is necessary, he unites himself with the soul of a particular individual ; and that he appears in various forms for the purpose of establishing *dharma*, and of rectifying matters on the plane of human life, if *adharma* gets the ascendancy. From the words he uses there is reason to suppose that the number of his own incarnations has been very great, more so than our books are willing to admit. He apparenlty refers to human incarnations; if the *janmas* or incarnations referred to are simply the recognised human incarnations of Vishnu, there would perhaps be only two incarnations before Krishna, Rama and Parasurama, for the *Matsya*, *Koorma*, *Varaha* and *Narasinha Avatars* were not, strictly speaking, human incarnations. Even Vamana was not born of human father or mother.

The mysteries of these incarnations lie deep in the inner sanctuaries of the ancient arcane science, and can only be understood by unveiling certain hidden truths. The human incarnations can however be understood by the remarks I have already made. It may be that this *Logos*, which has taken upon itself the care of humanity, has incarnated not merely in connection with two individuals whose history we see narrated in the Ramayana and the Mahabharata, but also perhaps in connection with various individuals who have appeared in different parts of the world and at different times as great reformers and saviours of mankind.

Again, these *janmams* might not only include all the special incarnations which this *Logos* has undergone, but might also perhaps include all the incarnations of that individual, who in the course of his spiritual progress finally joined himself, or united his soul with the *Logos*, which has been figuring as the guardian angel, so to speak, of the best and the highest interests of humanity on this planet.

In this connection there is a great truth that I ought to bring to your notice. Whenever any particular individual reaches the highest state of spiritual culture, developes in himself all the virtues that alone entitle him to an union with the *Logos*, and finally, unites his soul with the *Logos*, there is as it were, a sort of reaction emanating from that *Logos* for the good of humanity. If I am permitted to use a simile, I may compare it to what may happen in the case of the sun when a comet falls upon it. If a comet falls upon the sun, there is necessarily an accession of heat and light. So, in the case of a human being who has developed an unselfish love for humanity in himself. He unites his highest qualities with the *Logos*, and, when the time of the final union comes, generates in it an impulse to incarnate for the good of humanity. Even when it does not actually incarnate, it sends down its influence for the good of mankind. This influence may be conceived as invisible spiritual grace that descends from heaven, and it is showered down upon humanity, as it were, whenever any great Mahatma unites his soul with the *Logos*. Every Mahatma who joins his soul with the *Logos* is thus a source of immense power for the good of humanity in after generations. It is said that the Mahatmas, living as they are apart from the world, are utterly useless so far as humanity is concerned when they are still living, and are still more so when they have reached Nirvana. This is an absurd proposition that has been put forward by certain writers who did not comprehend the true nature of Nirvana. The truth is, as I have said, every purified soul joined with the *Logos* is capable of stimulating the energy of the *Logos* in a particular direction. I do not mean to say that in the scase of every Mahatma there is necessarily any tendency to *incarnate* for the purpose of teaching *dharma* to mankind—in special cases this may happen—. but in all cases there is an influence of the highest spiritual efficacy coming down from the *Logos* for the good of humanity, whether as an invisible essence, or in the shape of another human incarnation, as in the case of Krishna, or rather the *Logos* with reference to which we have been speaking of Krishna. It might be, that this *Logos*, that seems to have incarnated already on this planet among various nations for the good of humanity, was that into which the soul of a great Mahatma of a former *kalpa* was finally absorbed ; that the impulse which was thus communicated to it has been acting, as it were, to make it incarnate and re-incarnate during the present *kalpa* for the good of mankind.

In this connection I must frankly tell you, that beyond the mystery I have indicated there is yet another mystery in connection with Krishna and all the incarnations mentioned in this book, and that mystery goes to the very root of all occult science. Rather than attempt to give an imperfect explanation, I think it much better to lose sight of this part of the subject, and proceed to explain the teachings of this book, as if Krishna is not speaking from the stand-point of any particular *Logos*, but from that of the *Logos* in the abstract. So far as the general tenour of this book is concerned, it would suit any other *Logos* as well as that of Krishna, but there are few scattered passages, that when explained will be found to possess a special significance with reference to this mystery which they do not possess now.

An attempt will be made in the "Secret Doctrine" to indicate the nature of this mystery as far as possible, but it must not be imagined that the veil will be completely drawn, and that the whole mystery will be revealed. Only hints will be given by the help of which you will have to examine and understand the subject. This matter is however foreign to my subject ; yet I have thought it better to bring the fact to your notice lest you should be misled. The whole philosophy of this book is the philosophy of the *Logos*. In general Christ or Buddha might have used the same words as those of Krishna ; and what I have said about this mystery only refers to some particular passages that seem to touch upon the nature of Krishna's divine individuality. He himself seems to think there is a mystery, as you may see from the 9th verse.

In the tenth verse "*Mathbhavam*" means the condition of the *Logos*. Krishna says there have been several Mahatmas who have become *Eswaras*, or have united their souls completely with the *Logos*.

Turn now to chapter v, verses 14 and 15 :—

"The Lord of the world does not bring about or create karma or the condition by which people attribute karma to themselves ; nor does he make people feel the effects of their karma. It is the law of natural causation that works. He does not take upon himself the sin or the merit of any one. Real knowledge is smothered by delusion, and hence created beings are misled."

Here he says that *Eswara* does not create karma, nor does he create in individuals any desire to do karma. All karma, or impulse to do karma, emanates from *Mulaprakriti* and its *vikarams*, and not from the *Logos*, or the light that emanates from the *Logos*. You must look upon this light or *Fohat*, as a kind of energy eternally beneficent in its nature, as stated in the "Idyll of the White Lotus." In itself it is not capable of generating any tendencies that lead to *bandham*; but *ahankaram*, and the desire to do karma, and all karma with its various consequences come into existence by reason of the *upadhis* which are but the manifestations of that one *Mulaprakriti*.

Strictly and logically speaking, you will have to attribute these results to both of these forces. *Mulaprakriti* will not act, and is incapable of producing any result, unless energised by the light of the *Logos*. Nevertheless, most of the results that pertain to karma and the continued existence of man as the responsible producer of karma are traceable to *Mulaprakriti*, and not to the light that vitalizes it. We may therefore suppose that this *Mulaprakriti*, is the real or principal *bandhakaranam*, and this light is the one instrument by which we may attain to union with the *Logos*, which is the source of salvation. This light is the foundation of the better side of human nature, and of all those tendencies of action, which generally lead to liberation from the bonds of *avidya*.

Turn to chapter vii, verses 4 and 5 :—

"My *Prakriti* (*Mulaprakriti*) is divided into eight parts—earth, water, fire, wind, ether, mind, intuition and egotism. This *Prakriti* is called *Aparaprakriti*."

"Understand my *Paraparakrit* (*Daiviprakriti*,) as something distinct from this. This *Daiviprakriti* is the one life by which the whole Universe is supported."

Krishna in verse 5 distinguishes between this *Daiviprakriti* and *Parakriti*. This *Daiviprakriti* is, strictly speaking, the *Mahachaitanyam* of the whole cosmos, the one energy, or the only force from which spring all force manifestations. He says you must look upon it as something different from the *Prakriti* of the Sankhyas.

Turn now to chapter vii, verse 7 :—

"O Dhanamjaya, there is nothing superior to me, and all this hangs on me as a row of gems on the string running through them."

Please notice that in verses 4 and 5 Krishna is referring to two kinds of *Prakriti*. Of course that *Prakriti*, which is differentiated into the eight elements enumerated in Sankhya philosophy is the *avyaktam* of the Sankhyas—it is the *Mulaprakriti*, which must not be confounded with the *Daiviprakriti*, which is the light of the *Logos*. Conceive *Mulaprakriti* as *avidya*, and *Daiviprakriti*, the light of the *Logos*, as *vidya*. These words have other meanings also. In the Swetaswatara Upanishad *Eswara* is described as the deity who controls both *vidya* and *avidya*.

Here Krishna seems to refer to all the qualities, or all the excellent qualities, manifested in every region of phenomenal existence, as springing from himself.

No doubt the other qualities also or rather their ideal forms originally spring from him, but they ought to be traced mainly to *Mulaprakriti*, and not to himself.

I will now refer you to verse 24 and the following verses of the same chapter :—

" The ignorant, who do not know my supreme and indestructible and best nature, regard me as a manifestation of *avyaktam*.

" Veiled by my *yoga maya* I am not visible to all. The deluded world does not comprehend me, who am unborn and imperishable.

" I know, O Arjuna, all beings, past, present, and future, but none knows me."

In these verses Krishna is controverting a doctrine that has unfortunately created a good deal of confusion. I have already told you that the Sankhyas have taken their *avyaktam*, or rather *Parabrahmam* veiled by *Mulaprakriti*, as *Atma* or the real self. Their opinion was that this *avyaktam* took on a kind of phenomenal differentiation on account of association with *upadhi*, and when this phenomenal differentiation took place, the *avyaktam* became the *Atma* of the individual. They have thus altogether lost sight of the *Logos*. Startling consequences followed from this doctrine. They thought that there being but one *avyaktam*, one soul, or one spirit, that existed, in every *upadhi*, appearing differentiated, though not differentiated in reality, if somehow we could control the action of *upadhi*, and destroy the *maya* it had created, the result would be the complete extinction of man's self and a final *layam* in this *avyaktam*, *Parabrahmam*. It is this doctrine that has spoilt the Adwaiti philosophy of this country, that has brought the Buddhism of Ceylon, Burmah and China to its present deplorable condition, and led so many Vedantic writers to say that Nirvana was in reality a condition of perfect *layam* or annihilation.

If those who say that Nirvana is annihilation are right, then, so far as the individuality of the soul is concerned, it is completely annihilated, and what exists ultimately is not the soul, or the individual however purified or exalted, but the one *Parabrahmam*, which has all along been existing, and that *Parabrahmam* itself is a sort of unknowable essence which has no idea of self, nor even an individual existence, but which is the one power, the one mysterious basis of the whole cosmos. In interpreting the *Pranava*, the Sankhyas made the *ardhamatra* really mean this *Avyaktam* and nothing more. In some Upanishads this *ardhamatra* is described as that which, appearing differentiated is the soul of man. When this differentation, which is mainly due to the *upadhi*, is destroyed, there is a *layam* of *Atma* in *Parabrahmam*. This is also the view of a considerable number of persons in India, who called themselves Adwaitis. It is also the view put forward as the correct Vedantic view. It was certainly the view of the ancient Sankhyan philosophers, and is the view of all those Buddhists who consider Nirvana to be the *layam* of the soul in *Parabrahmam*.

After reaching *karana sarira* there are two paths, both of which lead to *Parabrahmam*. *Karana sarira*, you must know, is an *upadhi* ; it is material, that is to say, it is derived from *Mulaprakriti*, but there is also acting in it, as its light and energy the light from the *Logos*, or *Daiviprakriti* or *Fohat*. Now, as I have said, there are two paths. When you reach *Karana sarira* you can either confine your attention to the *upadhi* and, tracing its genealogy up to *Mulaprakriti*, arrive at *Parabrahmam* at the next step, or you may lose sight of the *upadhi*, altogether, and fix your attention solely upon the energy, or light, or life, that is working within it. You may then try to trace its origin, travelling along the ray till you reach its source, which is the *Logos* and from the standpoint of the *Logos* try to reach *Parbrahmam*.

Of these two paths a considerable number of modern Vedantists, and all Sankhyas and all Buddhists—except those who are acquainted with the occult doctrine—have chosen the one that leads to *Mulaprakriti*, hoping thus to reach *Parabrahmam* ultimately. But in the view taken by these philosophers the *Logos* and its light were completely lost sight of. *Atma*, in their opinion, is the differentiated appearance of this *avyaktam* and nothing more.

Now what is the result ? The differentiated appearance ceases when the *upadhi* ceases to exist, and the thing that existed before exists afterwards, and that thing is *avyaktam*, and beyond it there is *Parabrahmam*. The individuality of man is completely annihilated. Further, in such a case it would be simply absurd to speak of *Avatars*, for they would then be impossible and out of the question. How is it possible for Mahatmas, or adepts, to help mankind in any possible way when once they have reached this stage ? The Cingalese Buddhists have pushed this doctrine to its logical conclusion. According to them Buddha is extinguished, and every man who follows his doctrine will eventually lose the individuality of his *Atma*; therefore they say that the Tibetans are entirely mistaken in thinking that Buddha has been overshadowing, or can overshadow any mortals; since the time he reached Paranirvana the soul of the man who was called Buddha has lost its individuality. Now I say that Krishna protests against the doctrine which leads to such consequences.

He says (verse 24) that such a view is wrong, and that those who hold it do not understand his real position as the *Logos* or *Verbum*. Moreover he tells us the reason why he is thus lost sight of. He says it is so because he is always veiled by his *yoga maya*. This *yoga maya* is his light. It is supposed that this light alone is visible, the centre from which it radiates remaining always invisible.

As may naturally be expected this light is always seen mixed up, or in conjunction, with the Emanations of *Mulaprakriti*. Hence Sankhyas have considered it to be an aspect of, or an Emanation from *Mulaprakriti*. *Avyaktam* was in their opinion the source, not only of matter, but of force also.

But according to Krishna this light is not to be traced to *avyaktam*, but to a different source altogether, which source is himself. But, as this source is altogether *arupa* and mysterious and cannot be easily detected, it was supposed by these philosophers that there was nothing more in and behind this light, except their *avykatam* its basis. But this light is the veil of the *Logos* in the sense that the Shekinah of the Kabbalists is supposed to be the veil of Adonai. Verily it is the Holy Ghost that seems to form the flesh and blood of the divine Christ. If the *Logos* were to manifest itself, even to the highest spiritual perception of a human being, it would only be able to do so clothed in this light which forms its body. See what Sankaracharya says in his Soundaryalahari. Addressing the light he says :—"You are the body of Sambhu." This light is, as it were, a cloak, or a mask, with which the *Logos* is enabled to make its appearance.

The real centre of the light is not visible even to the highest spiritual perception of man. It is this truth which is briefly expressed in that priceless little book "Light on the Path," when it says (rule 12) :—" It is beyond you ; because when you reach it you have lost yourself. It is unattainable because it for ever recedes. You will enter the light, but you will never touch the flame."

You will bear in mind the distinction that Krishna draws between the unfortunate doctrine of the Sankhyas and others, and the true theory which he is endeavouring to inculcate, because it leads to important consequences. Even now I may say that ninety per cent. of the Vedantic writers hold the view which Krishna is trying to combat.

Turn now to chapter viii, and examine the meaning of verses 5 to 16.

In these passages Krishna lays down two propositions which are of immense importance to humanity. First, he says that the soul can reach and become finally assimilated with himself. Next, he says, that when once he is reached there is no more *Punarjanmam*, or rebirth, for the man who has succeeded in reaching him.

Against the latter proposition some objections have sometimes been raised. It is said that if the soul reaches the *Logos* and the spiritual individuality of the *Logos* is preserved, and yet if the *Logos* has also to overshadow mortals from time to time, or have any connection with a human being living on earth, then the statement that a man who reaches the *Logos* will have no *Punarjanmam* is untrue. But this objection arises from a misunderstanding as to the nature of this union with the *Logos*. As far as we know, judging from our ordinary experience, this individuality, this sense of Ego, which we have at present is a kind of fleeting entity changing from time to time. Day after day the different experiences of man are being stored up, and in a mysterious manner united into a single individuality. Of course it seems to every man that he has a definite individuality during the course of a particular incarnation, but the individuality of his *Karana Sarira* is made up of several individualities like these. It must not be imagined that all the experiences that are connected with the various incarnations and go to constitute their respective personalities are to be found in a kind of mechanical juxtaposition in the *karana sarira*. It is not so. Nature has a sort of machinery by which it is able to reduce all these bundles of experiences into a single self. Great as is this higher individuality of the human monad, there is an individuality over and above this and far greater than it is. The *Logos* has an individuality of its own. When the soul rises to the *Logos*, all that this latter takes from the soul is that portion of the soul's individuality which is high and spiritual enough to live in the individuality of the *Logos*; just as the *Karana Sarira* makes a choice between the various experiences of a man, and only assimilates such portions thereof as belong to its own nature, the *Logos*, when it unites itself with the soul of a man, only takes from it that which is not repugnant to its nature.

But now see what changes take place in the consciousness of the human being himself. The moment this union takes place, the individual at once feels that he is himself the *Logos*, the monad formed from whose light has been going through all the experiences which he has now added to his individuality In fact his own individuality is lost, and he becomes endowed with the original individuality of the *Logos*. From the standpoint of the *Logos* the case stands thus. The *Logos* throws, out a kind of feeler, as it were, of its own light into various organisms. This light vibrates along a series of incarnations and whenever it produces spiritual tendencies, resulting in experience that is capable of being added to the individuality of the *Logos*, the *Logos* assimilates that experience. Thus the individuality of the man becomes the individuality of the *Logos* and the human being united to the *Logos* thinks that this is one of the innumerable spiritual individualities that he has assimilated and united in himself, that self being composed of the experiences which the *Logos* has accumulated, perhaps from the beginning of time. That individual will therefore never return to be born again on earth. Of course if the *Logos* feels that It is born, whenever a new individual makes his appearance having its light in him, then the individual who has become assimilated with the *Logos* may no doubt be said to have *punarjanmam*. But the *Logos* does not suffer because its light is never contaminated by the *Vikarams* of *Prakriti*. Krishna points out that he is simply *Upadrishtha*, a witness, not personally interested in the result at all, except when a certain amount of spirituality is generated and the Mahatma is sufficiently purified to assimilate his soul with the *Logos*. Up to that time he says, "I have no personal concern, because I simply watch as a disinterested witness. Because my light appears in different organisms, I do not therefore suffer the pains and sorrows that a man may have to bear. My spiritual nature is in no way contaminated by the appearance of my light in various organisms." One might just as well say that the sun is defiled or rendered impure, because its light shines in impure places. In like manner it cannot be true to say that the *Logos* suffers. Therefore it is not the real self that feels pleasure or pain, and when a man assimilates his soul with the *Logos*, he no longer suffers either the pains or pleasures of human life.

Again when I speak of the light of the *Logos* permeating this cosmos and vibrating in various incarnations, it does not necessarily follow that a being who has gone to the *Logos* is incarnated again. He has then a well defined spiritual individuality of his own, and though the *Logos* is *Eswara*, and its light is the *Chaitanyam* of the universe, and though the *Logos* from time to time assimilates with its own spiritual nature the purified souls of various Mahatmas, and also overshadows certain individuals, still the *Logos* itself never suffers and has nothing like *Punarjanmam* in the proper sense of the word ; and a man who is absorbed into it becomes an immortal, spiritual being, a real *Eswara* in the cosmos, never to be reborn, and never again to be subject to the pains and pleasure of human life.

It is only in this sense that you have to understand immortality. If unfortunately immortality is understood in the sense in which it is explained by the modern Vedantic writers and by the Cingalese Buddhists, it does not appear to be a very desirable object for man's aspirations. If it be true, as these teach, that the individuality of man, instead of being ennobled and preserved and developed into a spiritual power, is destroyed and annihilated, then the word immortality becomes a meaningless term.

I think I have the complete authority of Krishna for saying that this theory is correct, and this I believe to be, though all may not agree with me on this point, a correct statement of the doctrine of Sankaracharya and Buddha.

Turn now to chapter ix, verse 11 :—

"The deluded, not knowing my supreme nature, despise me, the Lord (*Eswara*) of all beings, when dwelling in a human body."

Here Krishna calls himself the real *Eswara.* Again in verse 13 :—

"The Mahatmas devoted to *Daiviprakriti*, and knowing me as the imperishable cause of all beings, worship me with their minds concentrated on me."

Here he refers to *Daiviprakriti,* between which and *Mulaprakriti* he draws a clear distinction. By some however this *Daiviprakriti* is looked upon as a thing to be shunned, a force that must be controlled. It is on the other hand a beneficent energy, by taking advantage of which a man may reach its centre and its source.

See verse 18 of the same chapter :—

"I am the refuge, the protector, the Lord, the witness, the abode, the shelter, the friend, the source, the destruction, the place, the receptable, the imperishable seed."

All these epithets applied by Krishna to himself, show that he is speaking of himself in the same manner as Christ spoke of himself, or as every great teacher, who was supposed to have represented the *Logos* for the time being on this planet, spoke of himself.

Another very significant passage is verse 22 of the same chapter :—

"I take interest in the welfare of those men, who worship me, and think of me alone, with their attention always fixed on me."

I have told you that in the generality of cases Krishna, or the *Logos,* would simply be a disinterested witness, watching the career of the human monad, and not concerning itself with its interests. But, in cases where real spiritual progress is made, the way is prepared for a final connection with the *Logos.* It commences in this manner : the *Logos* begins to take a greater interest in the welfare of the individual, and becomes his light and his guide, and watches over him, and protects him. This is the way in which the approach of the *Logos* to the human soul commences. This interest increases more and more, till, when the man reaches the highest spiritual development, the *Logos* enters into him, and then, instead of finding within himself merely the reflection of the *Logos*, he finds the *Logos* itself. Then the final union takes place, after which there is no more incarnation for the man. It is only in such a case that the *Logos* becomes more than a disinterested spectator.

I must here call your attention to verse 29 and the following verses at the end of this chapter :—

"I am the same to all beings, I have neither friend nor foe; those who worship Me with devotion are in Me, and I am in them.

"Even if he whose conduct is wicked worships Me alone, he is to be regarded as a good man, for he is working in the right direction.

"O son of Kunti, he soon becomes a virtuous person, and obtains eternal peace; rest assured that my worshipper does not perish.

"Those who are born in sin and are devoted to Me, whether women, or Vaishyas, or Sudras, reach my supreme abode.

"How much more holy Brahmans and devoted Rajarshis, having come into this transient and miserable world, worship me!

"Fix thy mind on me, worship me, bow down to me: those who depend on me, and are devoted to me, reach me."

Here Krishna shows, by the two propositions that he is laying down, that he is speaking from a thoroughly cosmopolitan standpoint. He says, "No one is my friend : no one is my enemy." He has already pointed out the best way of gaining his friendship. He does not assume that any particular man is his enemy or his friend. We know that, even in the case of *rakshasas*, Prahlada became the greatest of *bhagavathas*. Krishna is thoroughly impartial in dealing with mankind and in his spiritual ministration. He says it does not matter in the least to him what kind of *asramam* a man may have, what kind of ritual or formula of faith he professes; and he further says, that he does not make any distinction between *Sudras* and *Brahmans*, between men and women, between higher and lower classes. His help is extended to all there is but one way of reaching him; and that way may be utilized by anybody. In this respect he draws a distinction between the doctrines of the *karmayogis* and his own teaching. Some people say that certain privileged classes only are entitled to attain Nirvana. He says this is not the case. Moreover he must be taken to reject by implication the doctrine of certain Madhwas, who say that all souls can be divided into three divisions. They say that there is a certain class of people called *Nityanarakikas*, who are destined, whatever they may do to go down to bottomless perdition: another class of people called *Mityasamsarikas*, who can never leave the plane of earth; and a third class, the *Inthamuktas*, who, whatever mischievous things they do, must be admitted into *Vaikuntham.* This doctrine is not sanctioned by Krishna. His doctrine further contains a protest against the manner in which certain writers have misrepresented the importance of Buddha *Avatar*. No doubt some of our Brahman writers admit that Buddha was an *Avatar* of Vishnu; but they say it was an *Avatar* undertaken for mischievous purposes. He came here to teach people all sorts of absurd doctrines, in order to bring about their damnation. These people had to be punished; and he thought the best way to bring about their punishment was to make them mad by preaching false doctrines to them. This view, I am ashamed to say, is solemnly put forward in some of our books. How different this is from what Krishna teaches. He says:—"In my sight all men are the same; and if I draw any distinction at all, it is only when a man reaches a very high state of spiritual perfection and looks upon me as his guide and protector. Then, and then only, I cease to be a disinterested witness, and try to interest myself in his affairs. In every other case I am simply a disinterested witness." He takes no account of the fact that this man is a Brahman and that one a Buddhist or a Parsee ; but he says that in his eyes all mankind stand on the same level, that what distinguishes one from another is spiritual light and life.

"He is who is sensible enough amongst men to know me, the unborn Lord of the world who has no beginning, is freed from all sins."

Now turn to the 3rd verse of the next chapter (chapter X) :—

Here he calls himself the unborn : he had no beginning : he is the *Eswara* of the cosmos. It must not be supposed that the *Logos* perishes or is destroyed even at the time of cosmic *pralaya*. Of course it is open to question whether there is such a thing as cosmic *pralaya*. We can very well conceive a solar *pralaya* as probable, we can also conceive that there may be a time when activity ceases throughout the whole cosmos, but there is some difficulty in arguing by analogy from a definite and limited system to an indefinite and infinite one. At any rate, among occultists there is a belief that there will be such a cosmic *pralaya*, though it may not take place for a number of years that it is impossible for us even to imagine. But even though there may be a cosmic *pralaya* the *Logos* will not perish even when it takes place ; otherwise at the recommencement of cosmic activity, the *Logos* will have to be born again, as the present *Logos* came into existence at the time when the present cosmic evolution commenced. In such a case, Krishna cannot call himself *aja* (unborn) ; he can only say this of himself, if the *Logos* does not perish at the time of cosmic *pralaya*, but sleeps in the bosom of *Parabrahmam*, and starts into wakefulness when the next day of cosmic activity commences.

I have already said in speaking of this *Logos*, that it was quite possible that it was the *Logos* that appeared in the shape of the first Dhyan Chohan, or planetary Spirit, when the evolution of man was recommenced after the last period of inactivity on this planet, as stated in Mr. Sinnett's book, "Esoteric Buddhism," and after having set the evolutionary current in motion, retired to the spiritual plane congenial to its own nature, and has been watching since over the interests of humanity, and now and then appearing in connection with a human individuality for the good of mankind. Or you may look upon the *Logos* represented by Krishna as one belonging to the same *class* as the *Logos* which so appeared. In speaking of himself Krishna says, (chapter x, verse 6) :—

> "The seven great Rishis, the four preceding Manus, partaking of my nature, were born from my mind; from them sprang (was born) the human race and the world."

He Speaks of the *sapta rishis* and of the Manus as his *manasa putras* or mind-born sons, which they would be if he was the so-called Prajapati, who appeared on this planet and commenced the work of evolution.

In all Puranas the Maharishis are said to be the mind-born sons of Prajapati or Brahma, who was the first manifested being on this planet, and who was called *Swayambhuva*, as he had neither father nor mother ; he commenced the creation of man by forming, or bringing into existence by his own intellectual power, these Maharishis and these Manus. After this was accomplished Prajapati disappeared from the scene ; as stated in Manu-Smriti, *Swayambhuva* thus disappeared after commencing the work of evolution. He has not, however, yet disconnected himself altogether from the group of humanity that has commenced to evolute on this planet, but is still the overshadowing *Logos* or the manifested *Eswara*, who does interest himself in the affairs of this planet and is in a position to incarnate as an *Avatar* for the good of its population.

There is a peculiarity in this passage to which I must call your attention. He speaks here of four Manus. Why does he speak of four? We are now in the seventh *Manwantara*—that of Vaivaswata. If he is speaking of the past Manus, he ought to speak of six, but he only mentions four. In some commentaries an attempt has been made to interpret this in a peculiar manner.

The word "Chatwaraha" is separated from the word "Manavaha" and is made to refer to Sanaka, Sanandana, Sanatkumara and Sanatsujata, who were also included among the mind-born sons of Prajapati.

But this interpretation will lead to a most absurd conclusion, and make the sentence contradict itself. The persons alluded to in the text have a qualifying clause in the sentence. It is well known that Sanaka and the other three refused to create, though the other sons had consented to do so; therefore, in speaking of those persons from whom humanity has sprung into existence, it would be absurd to include these four also in the list. The passage must be interpreted without splitting the compound into two nouns. The number of Manus will be then four, and the statement would contradict the Puranic account, though it would be in harmony with the occult theory. You will recollect that Mr. Sinnet has stated that we are now in the fifth root race. Each root race is considered as the *santhathi* of a particular Manu. Now the fourth root race has passed, or in other words there have been four past Manus. There is another point to be considerd in connection with this subject. It is stated in Manusmriti that the first Manu (Swayabhuva) created seven Manus. This seems to be the total number of Manus according to this Smriti. It is not alleged that there was, or would be another batch of Manus created, or to be created at some other time.

But the Puranic account makes the number of Manus fourteen. This is a subject, which, I believe, requires a considerable amount of attention at your hands; it is no doubt a very interesting one, and I request such of you as have the required time at your disposal, to try and find out how this confusion has arisen. The commentators try to get the number fourteen out of Manu. Of course an ingenious pandit can get anything out of anything, but if you will go into the matter deeply, it is quite possible we may be able to find out how the whole mistake has arisen, and if there is any mistake or not. Any further discussion of the subject at present is unnecessary.

Another interesting function of the *Logos* is indicated in the same chapter, verse 11 :—

> "I, dwelling in them, out of my compassion for them, destroy the darkness born from ignorance by the shining light of spiritual Wisdom."

Here he is said to be not only an instrument of salvation, but also the source of wisdom. As I have already said, the light that emanates from him has three phases, or three aspects. First it is the life, or the *Mahachaitanyam* of the cosmos ; that is one aspect of it ; secondly, it is force, and in this aspect it is the *Fohat* of the Bhuddhist philosophy ; lastly, it is wisdom, in the sense that it is the *Chichakti* of the Hindu philosophers. All these three aspects are, as you may easily see, combined in our conception of the *Gayatri*. It is stated to be *Chichakti* by Vasishta : and its meaning justifies the statement. It is further represented as light, and in the *sankalpam* that precedes the *japam* it is evoked as the life of the whole cosmos. If you will read carefully the "Idyll of the White Lotus," you will perhaps gain some further ideas about the functions of this light, and the help it is capable of giving to humanity.

I have now to call your attention to all those verses in chapter x that refer to his so-called *vibhuti*, or excellence.

He says "*Aham Atma*" (I am self,) because every self is but a manifestation of himself, or a reflection of the *Logos*, as I have already indicated. It is in that sense he is the *Aham* (I) manifested everywhere in every *upadhi*. When he says this he is speaking from the standpoint of the *Logos* in the abstract, and not from that of any particular *Logos*. The description of this *vibhuti* conveys to our minds an important lesson. All that is good and great, sublime and noble in this phenomenal universe, or even in the other *lokas*, proceeds from the *Logos*, and is in some way or other the manifestation of its wisdom and power and *vibhuti* ; and all that tends to spiritual degradation and to objective physical life emanates from *prakriti*. In fact there are two contending forces in the cosmos. The one is this *prakriti* whose genealogy we have already traced. The other is the *Daiviprakriti*, the light that comes down, reflection after reflection, to the plane of the lowest organisms. In all those religions in which the fight between the good and the bad impulses of this cosmos is spoken of, the real reference is always to this light, which is constantly attempting to raise men from the lowest level to the highest plane of spiritual life, and that other force, which has its place in *Prakriti*, and is constantly leading the spirit into material existence. This conception seems to be the foundation of all those wars in heaven, and of all the fighting between good and bad principles in the cosmos, which we meet with in so many religious systems of philosophy. Krishna points out that everything that is considered great or good or noble should be considered as having in it his energy, wisdom and light. This is certainly true, because the *Logos* is the one source of energy, wisdom and spiritual enlightenment. When you realize what an important place this energy that emanates from the *Logos* plays in the evolution of the whole cosmos, and examine its powers with reference to the spiritual enlightenment which it is capable of generating, you will see that this description of his *vibhuti* is by no means an exaggerated account of Krishna's importance in the cosmos.

Turn next to chapter xi.

The inferences I mean to draw from this chapter are these. First, that the *Logos* reflects the whole cosmos in itself, or, in other words, that the whole cosmos exists in the *Logos* in its germ. As I have already said, the world is the word made manifest, and the *Logos* is, in the mystical phraseology of our ancient writers, the *pasyanti* form of this word. This is the germ in which the whole plan of the solar system eternally exists. The image existing in the *Logos* becomes expanded and amplified when communicated to its light, and is manifested in matter when the light acts upon *Mulaprakriti*. No impulse, no energy, no form in the cosmos can ever come into existence without having its original conception in the field of *Chit*, which constitutes the demiurgic mind of the *Logos*.

The *Logos*, its light and *Mulaprakriti* constitute the real *Tatwatrayam* of the Visishtadwaitis, *Mulaprakriti* being their *Achit*, this light from the *Logos* their *Chit*, and the *Logos* being their *Eswara*.

There is yet another way of looking at these entities with which you ought to familiarize, yourselves. The whole cosmos, by which I mean all the innumerable solar systems, may be called the physical body of the one *Parabrahmam* ; the whole of this light or force may be called its *sukshma sarira* ; the abstract *Logos* will then be the *karana sarira*, while the *Atma* will be *Parabrahmam* itself.

But this classification must not be confused with that other classification which relates to the subdivisions of one only of these entities, the manifested solar system, the most objective of these entities, which I have called the *sthula sarira* of *Parabrahmam*. This entity is in itself divisible into four planes of existence, that correspond to the four *matras* in *Prana*, as generally described. Again this light which is the *sukshma sarira* of *Parabrahmam* must not be confounded with the astral light. The astral light is simply the *sukshma* form of *Vaiswanara*; but so far as this light is concerned, all the manifested planes in the solar system are objective to it, and so it cannot be the astral light. I find it necessary to draw this distinction, because the two have been confounded in certain writings. What I have said will explain to some extent why the *Logos* is considered as having *viswarupam*.

Again, if the *Logos* is nothing more than a *Achidrupam*, how is it that Arjuna, with his spiritual intelligence, sees an objective image or form before him, which, however splendid and magnificent, is, strictly speaking, an external image of the world? What is seen by him is not the *Logos* itself but the *Viswarupa* form of the *Logos* as manifested in its light—*Daiviprakriti*. It is only as thus manifested that the *Logos* can become visible even to the highest spiritual intelligence of man.

There is yet another inference to be drawn from this chapter. Truly the form shown to Arjuna was fearful to look at, and all the terrible things about to happen in the war appeared to him depicted in it. The *Logos* being the universe in idea, coming events (or those about to manifest themselves on the objective plane) are generally manifested long, it may be, before they actually happen, in the plane of the *Logos* from which all impulses spring originally. Bhishma, Drona and Karna were still living at the time Krishna showed this form. But yet their deaths and the destruction of almost their whole army seemed to be foreshadowed in this appearance of the *Logos*. Its terrible form was but an indication of the terrible things that were going to happen. In itself the *Logos* has no form; clothed in its light it assumes a form which is, as it were, a symbol of the impulses operating, or about to operate, in the cosmos at the time of the manifestation.

IV.

The subject of these lectures is a very vast and complicated one. I have endeavoured to compress the substance of my lecture within the required limits, expecting to go through the whole discourse in three days, but my calculations have failed, and I have hardly finished even the introduction. These lectures must necessarily remain imperfect, and all I could do in them was to lay before you a few suggestions upon which you should meditate.

A good deal will depend on your own exertions. The subject is very difficult; it ramifies into various departments of science, and the truth I have been putting forward will not be easily grasped, and I might not even have succeeded in conveying my exact meaning to your minds. Moreover, as I have not given reasons for every one of my propositions, and have not cited authorities in support of my statements, some of them might appear strange.

I am afraid that before you can grasp my real ideas, you will have to study all the existing commentaries on the Bhagavad Gita, as well as the original itself, according to your own light, and see besides this to what conclusions the speculations of the Western scientists and philosophers are gradually leading. You will then have to judge for yourselves whether the hypothesis which I have attempted to place before you is a reasonable one or not.

In my last lecture I stopped at the eleventh chapter of the book.

In that lecture I pointed out the various passages relating to the *Logos,* which I thought would support and justify the assertions I made in my preliminary lecture about its nature and its relation to mankind. I shall now proceed to point out the passages to which it is desirable to call your attention in the succeeding chapters.

In Chapter XII, to which I shall have to refer again in another connection, I have to ask your attention to the passages with which it commences. There Krishna points out the distinction between meditating and concentrating one's attention upon the *Avyaktam* of the Sankhyas and fixing the mind and relying upon the *Logos*.

I have already shown in what important respects the Sankhya philosophy differed from the Vedantic system of Krishna. Krishna has stated in various places, that their *Avyaktam* was different from his *Parabrahmam*—that he was by no means to be considered a manifestation of that *Avyaktam*—and now he tells Arjuna in this chapter that those who try to follow the Sankhya philosophy and endeavour to reach that *Avyaktam* by their own methods, are placed in a far more difficult position than those whose object is to search for and find out the *Logos*.

This must naturally be so, and for this reason. This *Avyaktam* is nothing more than *Mulaprakriti*. The Sankhyas thought that their *Avyaktam* was the basis of the differentiated *Prakrati* with all its *gunas*, this differentiated *Prakrati* being represented by the three principles into which I have divided the solar system. In case you follow the Sankhyan doctrine, you have to rise from *Upadhi* to *Upadhi* in gradual succession, and when you try to rise from the last *Upadhi* to their *Avyaktam*, there is unfortunately no connection that is likely to enable your consciousness to bridge the interval. If the Sankhyan system of philosophy is the true one, your aim will be to trace *Upadhi* to its source, but not consciousness to its source. The consciousness manifested in every *Upadhi* is traceable to the *Logos* and not to the *Avyaktam* of the Sankhyas. It is very much easier for a man to follow his own consciousness farther and farther into the depths of his own inmost nature, and ultimately reach its source —the *Logos*—,than to try to follow *Upadhi* to its source in this

Mulaprakriti, this *Avyaktam*. Moreover, supposing you do succeed in reaching this *Avyaktam*, you can never fix your thoughts in it or preserve your individuality in it ; for, it is incapable of retaining any of these permanently. It may be that to reach it means to take objective cognisance of it, but even that you cannot do from the standpoint of *karana sarira*. You have to rise to a still higher level before you can look upon *Mulaprakriti* as an object. Thus, considering *Avyaktam* as an object of perception, you cannot reach it until you reach the *Logos*. You cannot transfer your individuali ty to it, for the simple reason that this individuality derives its source from a quarter altogether different from the *Mulaprakriti* or the *Avyaktam* of the Sankhyas, and that as this *Avyaktam* in itself has no individuality, and does not generate by itself anything like an individuality, it is impossible that anybody's sense of ego can be transferred to and preserved permanently in it.

What, then, do the efforts of all those who try to follow the Sankhya doctrine end in ? Krishna says, that after arriving at the plane of *karana sarira*," they will come to him," finding it impossible otherwise to reach this *Avyaktam* for the reasons indicated above. So when Arjuna asks whether *Avyaktam* or the *Logos* is to be the goal, Krishna says that the latter must be looked upon as the ultimate destination, because those who try to follow the line indicated by the Sankhyas have tremendous difficulties to contend with. If anything is gained at all by following this latter course, it is that end which is also to be gained by following his path, by making him the object of meditation, and looking upon him as the ultimate goal.

Read Chapter XII, verses 3, 4, and 5 in this connection :—

" Those who are kind and charitable towards all creatures, and who, with a properly balanced mind and with senses under control, meditate on the imperishable and undefinable *Avyaktam*, which is all-pervading, unthinkable, undifferentiated and unchangable, reach me alone. But the difficulty of those who fix their minds on *Avyaktam* is great. The path towards *Avyaktam* is travelled by embodied souls under very great difficulties."

This description refers to the *Avyaktam* of the Sankhyas.

In Chapter XIII we find the following in the first four verses :—

" O son of Kunti, this body is called *Kshetra* (*Upadhi* or vehicle). That which knows this (*Kshetra*) the wise call *Kshetragna* (the real self or Ego).

" Know also that I am the *Kshetragna* in all *Kshetras* ; the knowledge of *Kshetra* and *Kshetragna* I consider to be real knowledge.

" Hear me. I shall state to you briefly what that *Kshetram* is, what its attributes are, what qualities it generates, its source and the reason of its existence ; and further who that *Kshetrayna* is, and what powers he possesses. Rishis have described them in various ways. Different accounts of them are to be found in different Vedas ; and they are also spokeu of by the Brahmasutras, which are logical and definite."

Here he speaks of *Kshetram* and *Kshetragna*. *Kshetram* means nothing more than *Upadhi* or vehicle, and *Kshetragna* is the Ego in all its forms and manifestations. *Kshetram* springs from this *Avyaktam* or *Mulaprakriti*. But he says that he himself is *Kshetragna* in the sense in which every manifested Ego is but a reflection of the *Logos*, while he himself is the real form of the Ego, the only true self in the cosmos. He takes care, however, to point out in several places that though he is *Kshetragna*, he is not subject to *Karmabandham* ; he does not create *Karma*, simply because the self manifested in the *Upadhi* is not his own true self, but merely a reflection, which has an individual phenomenal existence for the time being, but is ultimately dissolved in himself.

In verse 4 (see above) he refers to Brahmasutras for the details of the three *Upadhis* in man, their relation to each other and the various powers manifested by this Ego. Hence it is in that book—the Brahmasutras—that we have to look for a detailed examination of this subject.

Turn now to verse 22 :—

"The supreme *Purusha* in this body is called the Witness, the Director, the Supporter, the Enjoyer, the Great Lord and the Supreme Spirit (*Paramatma*)."

It must not be imagined that the word *Parmaatma* here used refers to *Parabrahmam.* I have already said that it applies to Krishna himself. Though he is *Kshetragna*, he is not responsible for *Karma*, and this he explains in verses 30 and 32 of the same chapter:

"He perceives the real truth who sees that *Karma* is the result of *Prakrit* and that the *Atma* performs no *Karma.*

"This imperishable and supreme *Atma*, does no *Karma* and does not feel the effects of *Karma* even while existing in the body, as it is without beginning and without *Gunam.*"

Throughout Chapter XIV Krishna distinctly repudiates any responsibility for *Karma*, or any of the effects produced by the three *Gunams* which are the children of *Mulaprakriti.* Look at verse 19 for instance :—

"When the (discriminating) observer recognizes no other agent (of *Karma*) than the qualities (of *Prakriti*), and knows that which is beyond these qualities, he attains to my being."

And now turn to the closing verse in that chapter, a passage we have already referred to in another connection :—

"I am the image of *Parabrahm*, which is indestructible, unchangeable; and (I am) the abode of the Eternal Dharma (Law) and of absolute happiness."

Here he says he is the image of *Parabrahmam* which is eternal and has no *Vikaram*, and he is the abode wherein resides the eternal *Dharma* of the cosmos, and he is also the abode of bliss, and it is for this reason that the *Logos* is often described as *Sachchidanandam.* It is *Sat*, because it is Parabrahmam; and *Chit*, because it contains within itself the eternal *Dharma* of the cosmos, the whole law of cosmic evolution; it is *Anandam*, because it is the abode of bliss, and the highest happiness possible for man is attained when the human soul reaches the *Logos.*

Now turn to Chapter XV, verse 7, a passage which has unfortunately given rise to many sectarian disputes :—

"It is the *amsa* which emanates from me and which is manifested from the beginning of time that becomes the *Jiva* in the world of living beings, and attracts mind and the other five senses which have their basis in *Prakriti.*"

The proposition herein made is a matter of necessary inference almost inevitable from the premises I have laid down :—if what constitutes the *Jiva* is the light of the *Logos,* which is *Chaitanyam,* and which, becoming differentiated, forms the individual Ego in combination with the *Karanopadhi.*

I need not now advert to all the controversies to which this passage has given rise. The verse is perhaps susceptible of more than one interpretation, and the different interpretations were necessitated by the different premises with which the interpreters started.

Read now verse 8 :—

"When the lord, *Jiva* (human Ego), quits one body and enters another he carries with him the mind and the senses as the wind carries the fragrance of flowers from their source."

Here Krishna refers to that human individuality which resides in the *Karana sarira.* It is the human monad or *Karana sarira,* that is the one connecting link between the various incarnations of man ; when it leaves the body for Devachan, it takes with it all the germs of conscious existence, the essence of the five *Tanmatras,* the *Manas* and the *Ahankaram.* Strictly speaking, in every stage of conscious existence, there are seven elements which are always present, viz., the five senses, the mind (also recognised as a sense by some of our philosophers), and the Ego. These are the seven elements that constantly manifest themselves whenever consciousness manifests itself, or conscious existence makes its appearance. They exist in the *sthula sarira*, further also in the *sukshma sarira*, and they are latent in *karana sarira*. Not only are they latent in *karana sarira*, but even the impulses generated in connection with the seven elements of conscious existence reside in it, and form that latent energy which tries to spend itself, as it were, by bringing about the future incarnations, the environments being those determined by the past *Karma* of the man and the impulses already generated thereby.

In calling attention to verses 12—14 :—

"Know that the splendour which belongs to the sun and illumines the whole word—which is in the moon and in fire—is from me.

"Entering into the earth, I sustain all things by my energy ; and I am the cause of the moisture that nourishes the herbs.

"Becoming fire (of digestion) I enter into the bodies of all that breathe, and being united with *Pranam* and *Apanam*, I cause food of the four kinds to digest."

I have only to point out that what Krishna really means is, that it is his energy that gives to matter all its properties, and that all the properties that we now associate with matter, and all those tendencies of chemical action that we see in the chemical elements, did not belong to it or them originally.

When you examine *Mulaprakriti* none of these tendencies are found to be present in it. It is simply the stuff or substance which is endowed with these properties by the action on it of the current of life which emanates from the *Logos*. Consequently Krishna says that all the qualities exhibited in matter, as in fire, the sun, light, or any other object that you may take into consideration, originally emanate from him, because it was his life, his energy, that gives to matter all the qualities that enable it afterwards to form the various organisms that we now see in the manifested cosmos. In connection with this point you will find it inter esting to refer to what is stated, I believe, in one of the ten Upanishads (Kenopanishad) with reference to the mysterious appearance of *Parasak ti (Daiviprakriti)* in *Swarga*.

When *Parasakti* first appeared, Indra wanted to know what it was. He first sent *Agni* to enquire what it was that appeared in that peculiar form. Then *Parasakti* asked *Agni* what functions he fulfilled or what was his latent capacities. *Agni* replied that he could reduce almost everything to ashes. And in order to show that this attribute did not originally belong to *Agni* but was simply lent to him, *Parasakti* placed before him a little bit of grass and asked him to reduce that to ashes. He tried his best, but failed. *Vayu* was next sent; but he also failed in a similar manner. All this was done to show that *Pararsakti*, or the light of the *Logos*, endows even the *Panchatanmatras* with qualities that did not originally belong to *Mulaprakriti*. Krishna is right in saying that he constitutes the real energy of the fire and of all those things he has enumerated.

Now turn to verse 16 of the same chapter, which has also given rise to a considerable number of interpretations :—

"These two *Purushas*—the perishable and the imperishable—exist in the world. The perishable is all the living beings, and the imperishable is called the *Kutastha*."

The meaning here is clear enough if you will only read it in the light of the explanations already given. Krishna first divides all existing entities into two classes, those not permanent—*ksharam*—by which he means the manifested cosmos, and *Aksharam*, or imperishable, which he calls *Kuthastham*, the undifferentiated *Prakriti*. He also uses the same word, in another passage, in connection with the *Avyaktam* of the Sankhyas; and it is but natural to conclude that he here uses the same word in the same sense.

In the succeeding verse he says that these two classes are

inferior to himself. Although *Aksharam* is not destroyed at the time of cosmic *Pralaya*, as are all the things that come out of it, yet his own nature is superior to that of this *Aksharam*, and that is why he is called *Uttama Purusha*. For we read in verse 17 : –

"But there is another, the supreme *Uttama Purusha*, called *Paramatma*) (the supreme Atma) who is the imperishable Lord, and who pervades and sustains the three worlds."

I have only to refer you, in this connection, to verse 66 of Chapter XVIII :—

"Renouncing all religious observances, come to me as the only refuge. I will deliver thee from all sins ; grieve not."

To crown all, here is a distinct declaration that he is the one means and the most effectual means of obtaining salvation. These are all the passages to which I wish to call your attention, in reterence to the *Logos*. The passages read go far, I believe to support every one of the propositions I have laid down in connection with it, as regards its own inherent nature and its relation to the cosmos and to man.

Now, as regards *Mulaprakriti*, I have already called attention to it in several places when speaking of *Parabrahmam* and of the *Logos*. There is one passage, however, which I did not cite. I believe I have clearly indicated the distinetion between this *Avyaktam* or *Mulaprakriti* and the *Logos*, as well as that between *Mulaprakriti* and *Daiviprakriti*.

I have also said that *Mulaprakriti* should not be confounded with *Parabrahmam*. If it is anything at all, it is but a veil of *Parabrahmam*. In order to support my statements I now ask you to turn to Chapter VIII, verse 20 :—

"But there is another *Avyaktam* superior to the *Avyaktam* above mentioned, which is without a beginning and which survives when all the *bhutams* perish."

The preceding verses should also be read :—

"At the approach of day all manifestations issue from *Avyaktam*: at the approach of night they are absorbed into *Avyaktam*.

"All these collective beings, produced again and again, are dissolved at the approach of night, O Partha (Arjuna), and are evolved involuntarily at the approach of day."

Here Krishna says that at the time when the cosmos wakes into a condition of activity, all the *bhutams* spring from this *Avyaktam*; when the time of *Pralaya* comes, they go back into *Avyaktam*. But lest this *Avyaktam* should be mistaken for *Parabrahmam*, he takes care to point out that there is an entity which is higher than this, which is also called *Avyaktam*, but which is different from the *Avyaktam* of the Sankhyas and even existing anterior to it. It is *Parabrahmam* in fact.

It is not an evolved entity, and it will not perish even at the time of cosmic *Pralaya*, because it is the one basis, not only of the whole cosmos, but even of this *Mulaprakriti*, which seems to be the foundation of the cosmos.

As regards *Daiviprakriti*, I have already called your attention to those passages in Chapter VII which refer to it.

Thus the four main principles I have enumerated, and which I described as constituting the four principles of the infinite cosmos, are described and explained, precisely in the manner I have myself adopted, in the teachings of this book.

Krishna does not go into the details of the four principles that exist in the manifested solar system, because, so far as the ultimate object of his teaching is concerned, it is not absolutely necessary for him to go into the details of that question, and as regards the relation of the microcosmic *Upadhis* to the soul and their connection with each other, instead of giving all the details of the philosophy connected with them, he refers to the Brahmasutras, in which the question is fully discussed.

The so-called *Prasthanathrayam*, upon the authority of which our ancient philosophers relied, composed of the Bhagavad Gita, the ten Upanishads and Brahmasutras, must be thoroughly examined to find a complete explanation of the whole theory.

The main object of the Bhagavad Gita--which is one of the main sources of Hindu philosophy—is to explain the higher principles that operate in the cosmos, which are omnipresent and permanent and which are common to all the solar systems.

The main object of the Upanishads is to indicate the nature of this manifested cosmos, and the principles and energies therein present.

Lastly, in the Brahmasutras an attempt is made to give a clear and consistent theory about the composition of the entity that we call a human being, the connection of the soul with the three *Upadhis*, their nature and their connection with the soul on the one hand, and between themselves on the other. These books are not, however, devoted to these subjects only, but each book deals prominently with one of these subjects, and it is only when you take all the three into consideration, that you will have a consistent theory of the whole Vedantic philosophy.

And now, granting the truth of the premises we have laid down, what are the conclusions that will necessary follow?

For this purpose the whole of the Bhagavad Gita may be divided into three parts. Of the first six chapters, the first is merely introductory, the remaining chapters deal with the five theories that have been suggested by various philosophers as pointing out to man the way to salvation; the succeeding six chapters explain the theory which Krishna advocates as pointing out the way which he recommends as the best one to follow, and give such explanations as are necessary. In the last six chapters, Krishna attempts by various arguments to point out that it is *Prakriti* which is mainly responsible for *Karma*, for even the various intellectual and moral qualities that are exhibited by human beings, for the varieties of the emotional nature, and for the various practices that are followed. It is impossible for me now to go into the whole of this argument in detail. In studying this book the last six chapters should be read first, because one of the main principles that will have to be taken into account in dealing with all the various measures that have been recommended, is therein enumerated and established; and our conclusions will have to be altered if the doctrine those six chapters are intended to inculcate is found to be false or untenable. Of course, in those six chapters, the illustrations are taken, not from matters with which we at the present day are familiar, but from matters which, at the time Krishna gave this discourse, were perfectly intelligible to his hearers, and to the public of that day, and with which they were thoroughly familiar. So it is possible that in the illustrations he gives we may not be able to find those arguments and those considerations, which, perhaps, a modern writer, trying to support the same conclusions, would present to the mind of the reader. Notwithstanding this, the nature of the argument is the same and the conclusion is true for all time to come. Illustrations will certainly be forthcoming, if necessary, from other departments of human knowledge with which we at the present day are familiar. It does not require any very lengthy argument to show, now that the works of Professor Bain and Herbert Spencer have been so widely read, that the human physical organism has a great deal to do with the mental structure of man; and, in fact, all modern psychology is trying to find a foundation for itself in physiology and is perhaps even going to extremes in this direction. The great French philosopher who originated what is called Positivism, would not, in his classification of sciences, assign a separate place to psychology. He wanted to give psychology a subordinate place, and include it, as a branch subject, under physiology.

This classification shows the extremes to which this tendency may lead. If all that is found in the body is nothing more than the material of which it is composed, true psychology is nothing more than physiology, and the mind is but an affection of matter. But there is something more than the mere physical organism ; there is this invisible essence that we call the supreme *Chaitanyam* which constitutes the individuality of man, and which is further that energy which manifests itself as the consciousness behind the individuality.

It is not material, and it is not likely, that science will be able to get a glimpse of its real nature till it begins to adopt the methods of all the great occultists who have attempted to probe into this mystery. But at any rate this much must be conceded; whatever the real nature of this essence or life-force may be, the human constitution or the physical body has a good deal to do with the mental development and character of a human being.

Of course the force that operates in all these *Upadhis* is, as it were, colourless—it can by itself produce no result. But when acting in conjunction with *Prakriti*, it is the force that is the substratum of all the kingdoms, and almost every thing in the cosmos is, in a certain sense, traceable to this force. When, however, you begin to deal with particular forms of conscious existence, particular characteristics and developments, you will have to trace them, strictly speaking, to the *Upadhis*, or the material forms in which the force is acting, and not to the force itself. So Krishna says all *Karma* is traceable to *Upadhi*, and hence to *Prakriti*. *Karma* itself depends upon conscious existence. Conscious existence entirely depends upon the constitution of the man's mind, and this depends upon the nerve system of the body and the various elements existing therein, the nature of the astral elements and the energies stored up in the *Karanopadhi*.

In the case of even the astral body the same law holds good. To begin with, there is the aura, which is material in the strict sense of the word, and which composes its *Upadhi*. Behind this there is the energy, which is the basis of that feeling of self that even an astral man experiences.

Going on still higher, to *Karana Sarira*, there again you find this invisible, colourless force acting within its *Upadhi*, which contains within itself the characteristics of the individual Ego.

Go where you will, you will find that *Karma* and the *gunams* emanate from *Prakriti* : *Upadhi* is the cause of *individual* existence.

Existence itself, I mean living existence, is however traceable to this light. All conscious existence is traceable to it, and furthermore, when spiritual intelligence is developed, it directly springs from it.

Now let us assume that this is the conclusion we are prepared to admit—and I need not enter into the details of the argument which you will find at length in the last six chapters. Let us now examine in order the various theories suggested by different philosophers. I shall take them as they are dealt with in the first six chapters of this book.

The first chapter is merely introductory. The second treats of Sankhya Yoga, the third of Karma Yoga, the fourth of Jnan Yoga, the fifth of Karmasanyasa Yoga, and the sixth deals with Atmasamyama Yoga.

These are the theories suggested by other philosophers, and in this list Krishna does not include that path of salvation pointed out by himself, which is set forth in the second group of six chapters. I believe that almost all the various suggestions made by different philosophers can be brought under one or the other of these headings. To complete the list there is the method suggested by Krishna himself as being of universal applicability and standing in the background, unknown and unseen, is that occult method, to facilitate which all the systems of initiation have been brought into existence. As this occult method is not of universal applicability, Krishna leaves it in the background and puts his doctrine in such a manner as to render it applicable to the whole of mankind. He points out the defects of each of the other systems, and takes, as it were, the best part of the five theories, and adds the one element, without which every one of these theories will become false. He thus constructs the theory which he recommends for the acceptance of mankind.

Take, for instance, the Sankhya philosophy. I have already explained the peculiar doctrine of the Sankhya philosophers that their *Avyaktam* itself was the one self-manifested everywhere in all *Upadhis*. That is more or less their *Puruhsa*. This *Purush* is entirely passive. It is not the *Eswara*, not the active creative God, but simply a sort of passive substratum of the cosmos, and all that is done in the cosmos is done by *Prakriti*, which produces all the organisms or *Upadhis* that constitute the sum total of the cosmos. They accept the view that *Karma* and all the results that spring therefrom are traceable to this *Maya* or *Prakriti*, to this substratum that forms the basis of all manifestation. Now it is through the action of this *Karma* that individual existence makes its appearance. On account of this *Karma* individual existence is maintained, and it is on account of *Karma* that man suffers all the pains and sorrows of earthly existence. Birth, life and death, and all the innumerable ills to which human nature is subject, are endured by mankind owing to this *Karma*. Granting their premises, if the ambition of your life is to put an end to all earthly sorrows, then your object should be to put an end to the operation of this *Karma*.

But the question is, how can you do this? While *Parabrah-*

mam remains passive, *Prakriti* goes on creating the cosmos without its interference. It is not possible to get rid of *Prakriti* or its *gunams* altogether. You may as well try to rid fire or, water of all its properties. Thus, *Karma* being the inevitable result of *Prakriti*, and *Prakriti* continuing to exist as long as you are a human being, it is useless to try to get rid of *Karma*. But, they say, you must try to get rid of the effects of *Karma* by reducing yourself to the passive state of existence in which *Parabrahmam* is, remaining simply a disinterested witness. Do *Karma*, not with a desire to do it, but from a sense of duty—because it must be done. The Sankhyas say : give up *Sangam*, that *desire* to do *Karma*, which alone seems to connect the soul with it, and renounce this connection, which alone renders the soul responsible for the *Karma*.

What will happen then ? They say, when you renounce this desire, *Karma* will become weaker and weaker in its ability to affect you, till at last you arrive at a condition in which you are not affected by *Karma* at all, and that condition is the condition of *Mukti*. You will then become what you were originally. You yourself are but a delusive manifestation of *Avyaktam*, and when once this delusive appearance ceases to exist, you become *Parabrahmam*.

This is the theory suggested by the Sankhyas. Furthermore, as this *Avyaktam*, which exists everywhere,—which is eternal, and cannot be affected by anything else—forms the real soul of man, to hold it responsible for any *Karma*, is shown in the chapter before us, to be but a figment of Arjuna's fancy. Self cannot kill self. All that is done by the real self is in reality what is done by the various forms of *Prakriti*. The one substratum is immutable and can never be affected by any action of *Prakriti*. For some inexplicable reason or other the one self seems to have descended from the condition of passive existence, and to have assumed a delusive active individual existence in your own self. Try to get rid of this delusive appearance, then the result will be that you attain Nirvana.

Krishna examines this theory. He admits two of the premises. He says that all this *Karma* is due to *Upadhi,* and leads to conditioned existence, subject to all the pains and sorrows of life. But he denies that the supreme end of man's life is to reach this *Avyaktam,* and he further states that it is far more difficult to reach this *Avyaktam* than to reach himself; and that even if those who direct all their efforts towards the attainment of this *Avyaktam* meet with any success at all, it can only be by joining him, for otherwise it is impossible to reach *Avyaktam.* While accepting two of the conclusions of the Sankhyas, he points out that the real goal is not the one they postulated.

Now let us turn to the second system. This is mainly that kind of philosophy which is inculcated by the followers of *Purva Mimansa.* Every form of ritualism has its basis in the philosophy of *Karmakanda.* The arguments here used by Krishna in support of his own conclusions will not be quite intelligible to our minds for the simple reason that times have changed during the last five thousand years. At the time this discourse was delivered, the Vedantic ritual was strictly followed, and the conclusions of the followers of *Purva Mimansa* were very well known and were a common topic of discussion. This philosophy was intended to provide a solution for all the difficulties that were common to the other systems of philosophy at that time evolved. But some of the arguments put forward by the Karma Yogis may be extended beyond the very limited form in which they are to be found stated in the books, and can be made applicable even to the life of modern times.

Karma Yogis say: True, this *Karma* may be due to *Upadhi*

but it is not due to *Upadhi* alone ; it is due to the effects porduced by the two elements *Upadhi* and *Chaitanyam*. Those philosophers who want to reject all *Karma* pretend to renounce it altogether. But that is an impossible task. No man, as long as he is a human being, can ever give up *Karma* altogether. He is at least bound to do that which the bare existence of his physical body requires, unless indeed he means to die of starvation, or otherwise put an untimely end to his life.

Supposing you do give up *Karma*—that is, abstain from it in action, how can you keep control over your own minds ? It is useless to abstain from an act and yet be constantly thinking of it. If you come to the resolution that you ought to give up *Karma*, you must necessarily conclude that you ought not even to think about these things. That being so, let us see in what a condition you will then place yourselves. As almost all our mental states have some connection with the phenomenal world, and are somehow or other connected with *Karma* in its various phases, it is difficult to understand how it is possible for a man to give up all *Karma*, unless he can annihilate his mind, or get into an eternal state of *Sushupti*. Moreover, if you have to give up all *Karma*, you have to give up good *Karma* as well as bad, for *Karma*, in its widest sense, is not confined solely to bad actions. If all the people in the world give up *Karma*, how is the world to exist ? Is it not likely that an end will then be put to all good impulses, to all patriotic and philanthropic deeds that all the good people, who have been and are exerting themselves in doing unselfish deeds for the good of their fellowmen, will be prevented from working ? If you call upon everybody to give up *Karma*, you will simply create a number of lazy drones and prevent good people from benefiting their fellow beings.

And, furthermore, it may be argued that this is not a rule of universal applicability. How few are there in the world who can give up their whole *Karma* and reduce themselves to a position of eternal inactivity. And if you ask these people to follow this course, they may, instead of giving up *Karma*, simply become lazy, idle persons, who have not really given up anything. What is the meaning of the expression "to give up *Karma?*" Krishna says that in abstaining from doing a thing there may be the effects of active *Karma*, and in active *Karma* there may be no real Karmic results. If you kill a man, it is murder, and you are held responsible for it; but suppose you refuse to feed your old parents and they die in consequence of your neglect, do you mean to say that you are not responsible for that *Karmà?* You may talk in the most metaphysical manner you please, you cannot get rid of *Karma* altogether. These are the arguments put forward by an advocate of this second view.

The unfortunate mistake that these Karma Yogis make is this; in their system there is little or nothing said about the *Logos*. They accept all the thirty-three crores of gods mentioned in the Vedas and say that the Vedas represent the *Logos* or *Verbum*. They say "the Vedas have prescribed a certain course to be followed, and it is not for you to say whether such a course is or is not capable of producing the result to be attained. You ought to take what is stated in the Vedas as absolute truth, and by performing the various rituals therein prescribed, you will be able to reach *Swargam*. Devas will assist your efforts, and in the end you will attain supreme happiness. That being the course prescribed, we are not called upon to give up all *Karma*, and thereby throw all existing institutions into a state of inextricable confusion."

To these Karma-vadis Krishna says: "One of your conclusions I accept, the other I deny. I admit that an incalculable number of evil consequences will follow as the result of telling people to give up *Karma*, but I cannot admit that your worship of the Devas is at all a desirable thing."

Who and what are these Devas? "They are beings on the plane of *Karana Sarira*. They can never give you immortality, because they are not immortal themselves. Even if through worshipping them you are enabled to reach *Swargam*, you will have to return thence into objective existence in a new incarnation. The happiness that *Swargam* can give you is not eternal and permanent, but subject to this disturbance. And what is more, if you worship the Devas, concentrating your mind on them and making them the sole object of your attention, it is their *bhavam* that you will obtain, and not mine." Taking all these circumstances into consideration, and admitting the many mischievous consequences that in their view will follow as the result of recommending every human being to give up *Karma*, Krishna adds to this system all that is to be found in the teaching that makes the *Logos* the means of salvation, and recommends man—if he would seek to obtain immortality, a method by following which he is sure to reach it, and not one that may end in his having to go through another incarnation, or being absorbed into another spiritual being whose existence is not immortal. Furthermore, all these thirty-three crores of gods spring into existence with the beginning of every *Manwantara* and disappear at *Pralaya*. Thus, when the very existence of the Devas themselves is not permanent, you cannot expect that your existence will become permanent by merging it into their plane of being.

I now turn to the third theory—*Karmasanyasa-Yogam*. This Krishna at once rejects as being a most mischievous and even impossible course to follow. All the advantages offered by its pursuit may be obtained by doing *Karma*, not as a matter of human affection, passion or desire, but as a matter of duty.

The fourth system is that of *Gnana Yogam*. When people began to perceive that Ritualism was nothing more than a physical act, and that it was altogether unmeaning, unless accompanied by proper knowledge, they said it was not the *Karma* suggested by the followers of *Purva Mimasa*, or the followers of any other particular ritual, that would be of any use for man's salvation but the knowledge of, or the intellectual elements underlying, the ritual that would be far more important than any physical act could be.

As Krishna says, their motto is, that all *Karma* is intended simply as a step to gain knowledge or *Gnanam*. These philosophers, while admitting that *Karma* should not be rejected, have prescribed other methods of their own, by means of which they thought salvation would be gained.

They said," Consider *Karma* to be a kind of discipline, and try to understand what this *Karma* really means. It is in fact merely symbolical. There is a deep meaning underlying the whole ritual that deals with real entities, with the secrets of nature, and all the faculties imbedded in man's *Pragna*, and its meaning must not be taken to apply to physical acts alone, for they are nothing more than what their outward appearances signify." In addition to mere *Karma yogam*, they adopted several other kinds of *yogam*, such as *Japam*. Strictly speaking, this *Karma-yogam* is not *yogam* at all, properly so called. They have added to it *Antar-yogam*, *Pranagnihotram*, and other things which may be more or less considered as refined substitutes for external ritual. Now as regards the theory of these philosophers. All that Krishna has to propose is that their *Gnanam* should be directed towards its proper source. They must have some definite aim before them in their search after truth, and they must not simply follow either *Japam* or *Thapas*, or any other method which is supposed to open the interior senses of man, without having also a complete view of the whole path to be traversed and the ultimate goal to be reached. Because, if the attainment of knowledge is all that you require, it may be you still stop short at a very great distance from the *Logos* and the spiritual knowledge that it can give you. Strictly speaking, all scientists, and all those who are enquiring into the secrets of nature, are also following the recommendations of this *Gnana-yogam.* But is that kind of investigation and knowledge sufficient for the purpose of enabling a man to attain im mortality? It is not by itself sufficient to produce this effect. This course may indeed ultimately bring to the notice of man all those great truths belonging to the principles operating in the cosmos, which alone, when properly appreciated and followed, will be able to secure to man the highest happiness he can desire—that is, immortality or *Moksham.* While admitting the advantages of the spirit of enquiry recommended by this school Krishna tries to direct it towards the accomplishment of this object.

Let us now examine the fifth system. The votaries of this sect, after having examined what was said by the Sankhyas as well as all the teachings of the other systems we have described, came to the conclusion that it would only be possible to give up *Karma* in truth and not merely in name, if you could somehow or other restrain the action of the mind. As long as you cannot concentrate the mind upon yourself, or turn self towards self, it is not possible for you to restrain your nature, and so long as you cannot do that, it is almost impossible to subdue *Prakriti* or rise superior to the effects of *Karma.*

These philosophers wanted men to act in accordance with certain recommendations they laid down as a more effectual and positive means of obtaining mastery over one's own mind, without which mastery they considered it impossible to carry out the programme of either the Sankhya or the *Gnana-yoga* schools.

It was for this purpose that all the various systems of *Hata-yoga* with their different processes, by means of which man attempted to control the action of his own mind, were brought into existence. It was these people who recommended what might be called *Abhiasa-yoga.* Whatever may be the definite path pointed out, whether *Hata-yoga,* or that department of *Raja-yoga* that does not necessarily refer to secret initiations, the object is the same, and the final purpose is the attainment of perfect control over oneself.

This recommendendation to practise and obtain self-mastery, Krishna accepts. But he would add to it more effectual means of obtaining the desired end,—means sufficient in themselves to enable you to reach that end. He points out that this *Abhiasa-yogam* is not only useful for training in one birth, but is likely to leave permanent impulses on a man's soul which come to his rescue in future incarnations. As regards the real difficulties that are encountered in following this system, I need not speak at present , because all of you are aware of the difficulties generally encountered by *Hata-yogis.* Many of our own members have made some efforts in this direction, and they will know from personal experience what difficulties are in the way.

Krishna, in recommending his own method, combines all that is good in the five systems, and adds thereto all those necessary means of obtaining salvation that follow as inferences from the existence of the *Logos,* and its real relationship to man and to all the principles that operate in the cosmos. He is certainly more comprehensive than any of the theories from which these various schools, of philosophy have started, and it is this theory that he is trying to inculcate in the succeeding six chapters.

As I have already referred to various passages in these six chapters to show in what light you ought to regard the *Logos,* I need not say anything more now, and if you will bear in mind the remarks I have already made, the meaning will not be very difficult to reach.

In this connection there is one point on which I have been asked to give some explanation.

Reference is made in this book to *Uttarayanam* and *Dakshinayanam* or day and night, or light and darkness. These are symbolical of the two paths *Pravrittimarga* and *Nivrittimarga*. What he calls *Uttarayanam* is *Nivrittimarga*, represented as day or the path of light, the path he recommends, and the other *Dakshinayanam* is *Pravrittimarga*, or the way which leads to embodied existence in this world.

But there is one expression in the book that is significant. Krishna says that those who follow this second path attain to *Chandramasamjyoti* and return thence, while those who follow the first method reach *Brahma*. This *Chandramasamjyoti* is in reality a symbol of devachanic existence The moon shines, not by its own light, but by the light derived from the sun. Similarly the *Karana Sarira* shines by the light emanating from the *Logos*, which is the only real source of light, and not by its own inherent light. That which goes to *Devachan* or *Swargam* is this *Karana Sarira*, and this it is that returns from *Devachan*. Krishna tries to indicate the nature of the *Logos* by comparing it to the sun or something that the sun symbolizes.

I may here draw your attention to one other contingency that may happen to man after death in addition to those I have already enumerated. Those who have read Mr. Sinnett's "Esoteric Buddhism" will, perhaps, recollect that he talks of the terrible fate that might befal the soul in what he calls the eighth sphere. This has given rise to a considerable amount of misunderstanding. The real state of things is that the *Karana Sarira* may, in very extreme circumstances, die, as the physical body or the astral body dies. Suppose that, in course of time, the *Karana Sarira* is reduced, by the persistence of bad *Karma*, into a condition of physical existence, which renders it imposible for it to reflect the light of the *Logos* ; or suppose that that on which it feeds, as it were,—the good *Karma* of the man—loses all its energy, and that no tendencies of action are communicated to it, then the result may be that the *Karana Sarira* dies, or becomes merely a useless aggregation of particles, instead of being a living organism, just as the physical body decomposes and becomes a dead body when the life principle leaves it.

The *Karana Sarira* may become so contaminated and so unfit to reflect the light of the *Logos* as to render any future individual existence impossible ; and then the result is annihilation, which is simply the most terrible fate that can befal a human being. Without proceeding further, I must stop here.

I beg that you will all kindly bear this in mind. We have merely commenced the study of Bhagavad Gita in these lectures. Try to examine, by the light of the statements found in our own books, and in modern books on Psychology and Science, whether the theory I have placed before you is at all tenable or not—decide for yourselves—whether that is the theory supported by the Bhagavad Gita itself. Do not rely on a host of commentaries which will only confuse you, but try to interpret the text for yourselves as far as your intelligence will allow, and if you think this is really a correct theory, try to follow it up and think out the whole philosophy for yourselves. I have found that a good deal more is to be gained by concentration of thought and meditation, than by reading any number of books or hearing any number of lectures. Lectures are utterly useless, unless you think out for yourself what they treat of. The Society cannot provide you with philosophical food already digested, as though you were in the ideal state of passivity aimed at by the advocates of the Sankhyan philosophy; but every one of you is expected to read and study the subject for himself. Read and gain knowledge, and then use what you have gained for the benefit of your own countrymen.

The philosophy contained in our old books is valuable, but it has been turned into superstition. We have lost almost all our knowledge. What we call religion is but the shell of a religion that once existed as a living faith. The sublime philosophy of Sankaracharya has assumed quite a hideous form at the present day. The philosophy of a good many Adwaitis does not lead to practical conduct. They have examined all their books, and they think with the Southern Buddhists of Ceylon, that *Nirvana* is the *Nirvana* promised by the Sankhya philosophers, and instead of following out their own philosophy to its legitimate conclusion, they have introduced by their *Panchayatana-puja* and other observances what seems to be a foolish and unnecessary compromise between the different views of the various sects that have existed in India. Visishthadwaita philosophy has degenerated, and is now little more than temple worship, and has not produced any good impression on men's minds. Madhwa philosophy has degenerated in the same manner, and has perhaps become more fanatical. For instance, Sankaracharya is represented in their Manimanjari as a Rakshasa of former times. In Northern India people generally recite *Saptasati* and many have adopted *Sakti* worship. Kali is worshipped in Calcutta more perhaps than any other deity. If you examine these customs by the light of Krishna's teachings, it must appear to you that, instead of having Hinduism, we have assimilated a whole collection of superstitious beliefs and practices which do not by any means tend to promote the welfare of the Hindu nation, but demoralize it and sap its spiritual strength, and have led to the present state of things, which, I believe, is not entirely due to political degeneration.

Our Society stands upon an altogether unsectarian basis ; we sympathize with every religion, but not with every abuse that exists under the guise of religion; and while sympathizing with every religion and making the best efforts we can for the purpose of recovering the common foundations that underlie all religious beliefs, it ought to be the duty of every one of us to try to enlighten our own countrymen on the philosophy of religion, and endeavour to lead them back to a purer faith—a faith which, no doubt, did exist in former times, but which now lives but in name or in the pages of forgotten books.